CHURCH

The CHURCH

Reflections from Paul's letter to the Ephesians

S. Robert Maddox

REDEFINING Faith RESOURCES

CHURCH

Published by Redefining Faith Resources

Cover: The Theater of Ephesus, Acts 19:23-41

Scripture quotations are from The Holy Bible, English Standard Version® (ESV®), copyright © 2001 by Crossway, a publishing ministry of Good News Publishers. Used by permission. All rights reserved.

ISBN-13: 978-1537419268

DEDICATION

In honor of John A. Holmquist

A valued friend.
His comprehensive understanding of the Church was
profound.
Great discussions; a rich analysis of the oneness found in
Christ.
He is now reaping the Heavenly reward.

CONTENTS

FOREWORD

SONS

"How many Muslims have made a decision to follow Jesus!?" I couldn't believe what I was hearing.

After almost ten years of living and working in the Middle East and North Africa, it appears the Spirit of God is being poured out all across the regions of the world with the heaviest concentration of Muslims. Missiologists indicate more people who formerly embraced Islam have placed their faith in Jesus in the last ten years than in the previous thirteen centuries.

A former colleague was updating me on the progress of proclaiming Christ. Apparently, there is now a group of Jesus followers in every village throughout an area previously untouched by the Good News. The movement had grown from several hundred believers to tens of thousands in just over a year.

Something comparable is seen in the early church.

While Paul was ministering in Ephesus, he wrote the church in Corinth about the success in ministry he was witnessing, "But I will stay in Ephesus until Pentecost, for a wide door for effective work has opened to me, and there are many adversaries." (1 Corinthians 16:8-9) In the midst of opposition, similar to the environment in most Muslim countries, he was effectively telling the story of Jesus.

Paul set up a school of ministry and trained others in the disciple-making process. He was so successful, the book of Acts records, "This continued for two years, so that all the residents of Asia heard the word of the Lord, both Jews and Greeks." (Acts 19:10)

Ephesus was an important harbor city. The missional church located here proclaimed a powerful life-changing message. The believers in Ephesus affected an entire region of the ancient world.

The letter Paul writes these Christ followers is important for us today. My dad, a fellow-minister, and life-long student, will undoubtedly provide insights you may not have previously considered.

I awoke countless mornings to him reading the Bible, underlining passages, connecting Scriptures, then spending time in prayer. As a man of the Word and the Spirit, he will guide you well through this important New Testament book.

May the church you lead, work in, or attend, change the world like the church in Ephesus. Like them, may all the residents surrounding your church be eternally impacted by the story of Jesus.

Zach Maddox
Lead Pastor
Connection Point Church
West Lafayette, Indiana

Stories have always enamored me. In the movie, *Road to Perdition*, Tom Hanks has two sons and his oldest son witnesses a crime. When asked if his son can keep it a secret, all he answers is, "He's my son."

I grew up a pastor's kid, predominantly in the Chicago area. I love my dad and always wanted to be with him. That meant I was always at the church. I was essentially Samuel (referring to the prophet in the Old Testament), living and sometimes sleeping at the church. I'm pretty sure I drove every administrative assistant completely bonkers (special apologies to Chris and Darlene for that phase when I thought I was a good drummer). After getting a worker's permit, since I was only 13 years old, I ended up getting a job at the church. I was their greens keeper and a sanitation engineer of a multi-level complex. In other words, I mowed the grass and was a janitor/custodian/whatever-you-want-me-to-do staff person.

In the movie, Tom Hanks ends up on the run with his son. In conversation, the son learns how much he is like his father. Thankfully, I have not witnessed a crime in which my dad had to cover my back, nor did I ever have to go on the run with him. But I, too, am a lot like my dad. He taught me how to serve others, work hard, give, love God, love the church, and love everybody.

Today, people tend to think of buildings when they hear the word *church*, but the church is people. This is especially hard for someone like myself to understand since I am task-oriented and more purpose-driven than people-driven. I live in the paradox where people are our purpose and my dad taught me accomplishing this means living beyond myself, both in serving and in faith.

It is fitting that this book is on Ephesians, as one of my favorite passages/prayers is "Now to Him who is able to do exceedingly abundantly above all that _we_ ask or think, according to the power that works in _us_…" I think we can miss that Paul is referring to the corporate church and not just us individually.

Mercedes-Benz has the motto *das Beste oder nichts*, which means *The Best or Nothing*. If my dad ran the company, the motto would change to, "The Best and Nothing isn't an option" (I won't bother with the German translation, although my mom's heritage would probably appreciate it). Today, I have the same mindset. When we have a Savior who gave His all, why give anything less than our best?

The biblical examples my dad always gave were, "It

isn't I who lives, but Christ who lives in me," and "To do all things, not unto man, but as unto the Lord."

A testimony of these examples is that I'm still always at the church, deeply passionate about the church, and have a deep love for the bride of Christ, the church. So much so that *my* kids love the church and always want to be at it. Today, I, too, am a pastor. I've had the privilege and opportunity to be a part of many great churches, especially the church I currently serve, James River Church. All of this wouldn't be possible without my dad who made more sacrifices for us than we will ever know (like selling his saxophone so that I could have braces) The majority of his English/Welsh heritage is evident in my humor and my teeth.

So, if you asked me about this book or any of my dad's previous books, my only response to you would be:

He's my Dad

Stephen Maddox
Producer/Technical Director/Associate Pastor
James River Church
Ozark, Missouri

INTRODUCTION

CHURCH LIFE

I was in the Spirit on the Lord's day, and I heard behind me a loud voice like a trumpet saying, "Write what you see in a book and send it to the seven churches, to Ephesus and to Smyrna and to Pergamum and to Thyatira and to Sardis and to Philadelphia and to Laodicea." Then I turned to see the voice that was speaking to me, and on turning I saw seven golden lampstands, and in the midst of the lampstands one like a son of man, clothed with a long robe and with a golden sash around his chest. The hairs of his head were white, like white wool, like snow. His eyes were like a flame of fire, his feet were like burnished bronze, refined in a furnace, and his voice was like the roar of many waters. In his right hand he held seven stars, from his mouth came a sharp two-edged sword, and his face was like the sun shining in full strength ... As for the mystery of the seven stars that you saw in my right hand, and the seven golden lampstands, the seven stars are the angels of the seven churches, and the seven lampstands are the seven churches. (Revelation 1:10-16, 20)

An old *Irish ditty* gives an interesting portrayal of church life: "*To live above with the saints we love; ah, that will be glory! But to live below with the saints we know, now that's another story.*"

The church is a divinely inspired covenant-community, referred to as "the body of Christ" (1 Corinthians 12:27) and having a relationship with Jesus similar to marriage. (Ephesians 5:23,32) One aspect of marriage is loving the spouse while overlooking unusual practices.

I have a tendency to invert my socks when removing them from my feet, which annoys my wife. My wife has a tendency to squeeze the toothpaste tube in the middle instead of the end, which annoys me. Yet love covers an abundance of annoyances, a "multitude of sins." (1 Peter 4:8)

How does marriage relate to church life? If people viewed marriage like several evaluate church, no one would be married for very long.

Many are far too critical of the church. Some become unnecessarily cynical. Believers are looking for a church that has never existed, a church where everything runs smoothly all the time.

Consider what Luke wrote about the early church: Acts 2 records the outpouring of the Holy Spirit, days of power; Acts 3 and 4 describes supernatural miracles, days of amazement; Acts 5 gives testimony of everyone living in harmony and hundreds committing their lives to Christ, days of growth; yet, Acts 6 chronicles a complaint among believers about the uneven distribution of provisions, *days of conflict*. Intermingled with divine blessings is human strife.

Many New Testament writings deal with elements of measurable discord. Some letters would not even exist had there not been contention in the early church.

Can an occasional season of conflict be healthy? Conflict is simply a means of communication; identifying differences of opinion, forcing better strategies, and creating more workable structures. Conflict should never cause alarm. When resolved, advancement normally follows.

Among the different interactions linked with church life, every follower of Jesus can expect these three.

Expect problems

Problems come for a variety of reasons.

An increase in attendance causes tension; a good problem. When more people attend, additional needs develop. Adjustments must occur and an element of uncomfortableness festers.

The last year of overseeing a church in Minnesota saw a lot of new people starting to join. These were days full of excitement.

The congregation had been founded by the efforts of two sisters in 1939. Having never married, the church became their child. They faithfully sat at every service in the third row from the front and closest to the middle aisle. As the matriarchs of the congregation, no one ever challenged or interfered with their seating preference.

The ushers did a great job helping new people find a place to sit. They filled every empty space, making everyone feel good about being crammed next to a total stranger. People were generally happy.

One Sunday, a newly-trained usher made the mistake of asking these elderly sisters to slide over to accommodate some guests. Seasoned ushers knew this was taboo. Fortunately, the visitors were not paying attention to these dear women. The look they were getting would have killed them and a funeral service would have been conducted instead of a worship gathering.

People function best when there is order. Every time changes occur to accommodate pressing needs, a season of confusion usually follows. No matter how good the plans, or how well they are implemented, some chaos is inevitable.

When new people start to attend, these *strangers* make long-time attendees feel like, "It's not my church anymore." This leads to problems. Influential members lose an element of power, created by the newer people not knowing or appreciating their sacrifice of service.

Hopefully, everyone will see the good from more people attending but they threaten a prominent member's sense of control.

Problems also come because people can become easily offended. Most attempt to be considerate of others and there is no justifiable reason for being unkind, yet some are far too easily insulted and others become troubled by everything.

In God's providence of creating various personalities, some need more affirmation than others. This is not a character flaw but rather a behavioral trait. Problems develop when these dear saints are not affirmed to unrealistic expectations.

Problems also come because of cross-cultural differences. In every church are people with various cultural backgrounds, different religious experiences, and dissimilar dispositions. This can make for rough waters. Although hard to comprehend, there are even some who are not happy unless some kind of controversy is stirring.

A church can be compared to an old-fashion rock tumbler. Various rocks, in difference shapes and sizes, are placed in the container. The constant motion causes the rocks to knock against each another, removing sharp edges. God uses the "one another" (John 15:12) principle to chip away carnal rough spots. Unfortunately, many *rocks* leap out of the tumbler before the polishing is complete. If this happens, more rough experiences are in the making, just waiting for them to re-engage.

Problems should not cause alarm. Flaws must be addressed and church life is a major vehicle for addressing them.

Problems also come on account of different levels of spiritual formation. Some following Jesus have not advanced very far in the faith, which is not measured by time, age, or years but by maturity. To intensify the problem, some who are more developed think it is their obligation to condemn those not advancing.

In a healthy human body, cells are at different stages of change. Similarly, in a healthy church, people are at different levels of spiritual formation.

Consider the issues prompting Paul to write to the Corinthians. They had major problems. Reading his first letter to them reveals division, immorality, inappropriate attitudes, abuse of spiritual liberties, improper dress, and misapplication of spiritual gifts. The church was completely messed up, yet not beyond God's ability to correct.

Wherever there are believers there will be problems and Jesus can rectify them all. If you are looking for a place that is peaceful and serene then go to a cemetery. The only place where things are perfectly calm is among the dead.

Expect more problems

Just when things appear to be working more smoothly, problems take on a new look. Some problems really do not end; they simply change like a chameleon to better blend in and hide. Is this a major reason why God places leaders in the church, to guide believers through the landmines of chronic and perpetual difficulties?

"Where there are no oxen, the manger is clean, but abundant crops come by the strength of the ox." (Proverbs 14:4)

This proverbial nugget took on greater meaning while helping a friend on his dairy farm. Behind the stalls where the cows were housed was a very long trench. I wondered why until the farmer grabbed a scoop and started cleaning out the ditch holding the "strength of the ox." Without cows in the stalls, the trench would have been clean, neat, and tidy. However, the abundance of milk does not come without unpleasant odors and messes. In the same way, an eternal harvest of souls will not happen without some stink to clean up. Church leaders are like farmers with a shovel, cleaning up the residue of strength.

Not only does change often come hard but some people refuse to change at all, leading to more problems. Two major misconceptions exist in the minds of many believers. First, the church is not about stability but change. Believers are being changed into His image from one degree of glory to another. (2 Corinthians 3:18) In an unstable world, people need stability yet steadiness is found in Jesus, not the Church.

Secondly, the church is not about growth but

transformation. Transformation involves becoming new, the Holy Spirit being the Renewing Agent. Church is about people getting right with the Lord, drawing closer to Jesus, and being filled with the Spirit. Believers are supposed to be transforming for the better. When they refuse, it only leads to more problems.

Expect Jesus

Were you expecting to read: *expect even more problems*? This may very well be, yet Jesus can solve them all.

The final book of the New Testament begins by describing the glorified Christ. John reveals Jesus as He is today; full of splendor and majesty. His awesome nature is seen, along with His power and might.

After this revelation, Jesus writes to seven churches in Asia. The churches receive from Him both compliments and corrections. After giving an encouraging word, He then tells them where improvement is needed. He mentions issues such as lost love, complacency, false beliefs, phoniness, self-sufficiency, conceit, and smugness. In other words, He addresses each church's true-to-life dilemma.

Where was Jesus in these seven problematic churches? Right in the middle! "And in the *middle* of the lampstands I saw one like a son of man.... the seven lampstands are the seven churches." (Vs. 13, 20)

Believers witness in church life the way the Lord

unravels complications and resolves differences. As those following Jesus are brought into the solving process of the covenant-community, they learn how He can disentangle personal issues.

Jesus has a solution for every situation you face. The problems in church life expose you to His tactics for settling difficulties, showing you how to handle the setbacks you encounter every day.

The church

To everyone seeking the Son of God, He is found in the church, even with all her problems. The church is the only delivery system provided by God for salvation.

Even with her many imperfections and glitches, Jesus loves the church. Occasionally believers get bent out of shape over some silly situation and think God is going to "blow the church out of the water." Nothing could be further from the truth. The church is His bride and He hates divorce; the church is His body and He is opposed to suicide.

God loves the church! His kingdom effectively advances only when His followers identify with one another in Christ. If someone does not love the church, they are not loving what He loves and are out of His will.

Out of a love for God, develop a greater love for the covenant-community that Jesus gave His life to save. Every church will have flaws but she is on an eternal journey and has not arrived at her final destination.

These reflections of Paul's letter to the Ephesians can help you gain a better understanding, a greater appreciation, and a truer love for the church. As the old gospel song accurately declares, "'Tis a glorious church, without spot or wrinkle, washed in the blood of the Lamb." The Savior has made her triumphant and beautiful, wonderfully forgiven by His atoning sacrifice on Golgotha's hill.

The final revelation of Scripture shows a brightly shining church, graciously illumined by His presence. (Revelation 1:13)

CHAPTER ONE

COMMUNITY

Paul, an apostle of Christ Jesus by the will of God, to the saints who are in Ephesus, and are faithful in Christ Jesus: Grace to you and peace from God our Father and the Lord Jesus Christ. (Ephesians 1:1-2)

When my wife and I lived in a southern suburb of Chicago, we decided to visit Holland, Michigan. Brenda had wanted to see this town since her childhood. We went during their weeklong annual Tulip Festival. The celebration is clearly a mainstay of the community.

The day we visited included a *Kinder Parade*. Every child in town was in the procession, many in Dutch costumes and wooden shoes. Whether they were from public, private, or home school, they walked behind a banner and waved to the spectators standing alongside the street. The marching bands from middle and high schools filled the route with music. The whole town came out to view the scene.

We watched this hour and a half parade, even though we did not know anyone participating. Why? Because we had not experienced what we were witnessing in such a very long time, a sense of community. The town was showing all the signs of having a long and prosperous future. They understood the importance of special occasions and giving time to one another.

A major core value of the church is being a covenant-*community*. Churches often measure their worth by the size of a crowd at various exciting events. Have they mistaken the *crowds* to be the same as a *community*? Attention grabbing occasions are needed but must be seen as only a single, sometimes minor, component. Whenever a congregation emphasizes crowd and downplays community, a sense of significance becomes lost.

The church my wife and I helped launch on the west side of Rapid City, South Dakota included the word "community" in the title. Church is more than a *building* on a street corner but a *gathering* of devoted followers of Jesus, living at their best when functioning around the core value of *one another*.

The Ephesians' Letter was written by someone who was instrumental in the church's establishment, helping them to grasp the meaning of their existence. Paul was inspired to show the association Jesus has with those identifying with His name, and how they achieve their purpose when serving as a heavenly conduit, streaming people to God from every nation.

The letter was prayerfully created as Paul was waiting for an appeal to Caesar, under house arrest and monitored by a guard. (Acts 28:16,30) Luke's historical narrative mentions Paul visiting Ephesus on more than one occasion. He personally ministered to them for three years and guided them into the empowerment of the Holy Spirit, confirmed by an evidential sign. On one of his trips to Jerusalem he met the elders of the church in a distant city, Miletus, and instructed them. He was a special friend and spiritual mentor, possessing a unique burden for this band of believers.

The town of Ephesus was located in a broad valley close to the Mediterranean Sea in the present-day country of Turkey, a large and beautiful metropolis having white houses and long streets with over 300,000 inhabitants, the fourth largest city of the Roman Empire.

Ephesus was an important commercial municipality and shipping center. The great attraction drawing visitors from all parts of the world was the temple of Artemis, originally a Greek goddess of hunters. She became a symbol of fertility, a sex goddess, encircled and served by 1,000 prostitutes. Her shrine was described as one of the seven wonders of the ancient world.

Sex, as well as religion, was big business in town. (Acts 19:23-25) Those following Jesus were constantly exposed to temptations. A pure lifestyle was in serious jeopardy. Paul helped his friends learn how to live in a city given over to paganism. His letter deals with issues such as a fascination with power (2:1-3), emptiness and licentiousness (4:17-19), depravity, drunkenness, and indecent desires (5:3ff). He provides a clear warning to every generation about the danger of compromise.

The climate in which this letter was written is not much different than today. Domination and control are highly valued. Decadence is big business, void of refined endeavors and right moorings. More and more people are living empty lives, some floundering in lewdness, liquor, and lust. Centuries ago, in the midst of similar circumstances, a dynamic church was birthed and flourished, causing an enormous life-altering impact throughout the region. Is this still possible?

The first two verses serve as a salutation yet also introduce the catalyst of church life. Paul presents two vital components, critical ingredients for transforming a city, making possible the fulfillment of her purpose.

Divinely called leaders

"Paul, an apostle of Christ Jesus by the will of God." (V.1) More is written about various kinds of leaders later, but the letter begins by acknowledging leadership. Congregations are to recognize divinely sent individuals as possessing a special commission to lead. These individuals have devoted their lives to the call of God and to serving Him.

During the Judge era in the history of Israel, three stories describe living conditions: An idolatrous family procured a private and personal priest; a man's wife was lavished upon and murdered; and, civil unrest broke out throughout the land. (Judges 17-21) The period was known for religious, moral, and civil anarchy.

In each story, a summary phrase is repeated, showing why individualism ruled and chaos prevailed: "In those days there was no king in Israel. Everyone did what was right in his own eyes." (Judges 17:6, 18:1, 19:1, 21:25)

In a vibrant covenant-community, there is leadership. Leaders in the local church focus on *overseeing* and are often referred to as *pastors* or *bishops*. Their primary responsibility is acquiring utmost sensitivity to the leading of the Holy Spirit.

When Paul spoke to the responsible individuals of the Ephesians' church at Miletus, he testified, "Pay careful attention to yourselves and to all the flock, in which the Holy Spirit has made you overseers, to care for the church of God, which he obtained with his own blood. I know that after my departure fierce wolves will come in among you, not sparing the flock; and from among your own selves will arise men speaking twisted things, to draw away the disciples after them. Therefore be alert, remembering that for three years I did not cease night or day to admonish every one with tears." (Acts 20:28-31)

A difference exists between *hirelings* and *shepherds*. What occurs when a hireling gives oversight to a flock? Jesus said, "He who is a hired hand and not a shepherd, who does not own the sheep, sees the wolf coming and leaves the sheep and flees, and the wolf snatches them and scatters them." (John 10:12) Hirelings forsake the group.

The salutation to the Ephesians highlights the importance of a *divine call* upon leaders. Vocational ministry is not an occupational choice (hireling) but a divinely mandated work (shepherd). Paul was an *apostle*, someone appointed for a particular duty, having a marked mission from the Lord.

The greeting also reveals Paul's leadership is "by the will of God." Does this suggest the congregation agreed with him; they were in *one accord* that he was sent by God to help them? (Acts 4:32-33; 5:12; 8:6) What links someone's divine call to a particular church?

A critical question must be answered: Is it God's will for a local church to be part of a certain person's missional assignment? A group is not attempting to scrutinize a leader's special calling to serve the Lord, they are affirming that the call includes leading them. Harmony is necessary for both the leader and covenant-community to benefit from a divine appointment.

Aspiring churches have overseers, commissioned by God, serving as leaders. No congregation can clearly illuminate the message of Christ without a light-shining torchbearer.

Devoted saints

"To the saints who are in Ephesus, and are faithful in Christ Jesus." (V.1) The expression *saints* indicate people sincerely devoted to a holy God. Sainthood does not start after physical death. Every follower of Jesus carries the designation the moment they are *born from above*. (John 3:3)

A primary focus in the salutation is the *faithfulness* of these people. A covenant-community is established by *devoted followers* of Jesus, saints committed to one another and *not* ruled by "my way, no way, or the highway."

The kingdom of God sees little advancement when believers have personal agendas. In every local assembly, a few people *run alongside* yet do not *enter in*. If not in control, they are uncomfortable. Everything must fit within personal parameters. How can a unified mission advance when this attitude prevails? Only when everyone is *part of the bunch* will selfish supremacy not exist.

Saints who are faithful do not let incidental issues sidetrack the cause of Christ. They are people maintaining a *helpful* instead of *useless* attitude. Their mission is to spiritually strengthen and personally encourage others serving Christ.

When pastoring the Stone Church of Chicago Southland, I was often asked the size of the congregation. A hard question to answer! Define *congregation*? I knew how many attended on an average Sunday morning, yet I could only estimate how many crossed over from the *crowd* and became a faithful part of the *community*. The number of *faithful* ones sincerely building up the body of

Christ was virtually incalculable. No doubt, *grumblers* were also hiding behind the scenes and tearing down the covenant-community. The best light-bearing church is comprised of devoted saints dedicated beyond minor annoyances, having a strongly rooted faith in Jesus.

Grace and peace

"Grace and peace to you from God our Father and the Lord Jesus Christ." (V.2) The combination of *commissioned leaders* and *faithful saints* brings a sense of *unmerited favor* into a covenant-community.

Grace means receiving something completely undeserved. Out of unwarranted love, spiritual benefits are witnessed, special provisions are supplied, and supreme empowerment is manifested. These traits are not deserved and gratefulness is abundant.

Peace means enjoying inner tranquility, a covenant-community undisturbed by occasional turmoil. Contention, conflict, and controversy are left outside the gatherings. Healing becomes available for troubled minds and broken hearts. Lives become eternally restored and refreshed. New hope, new faith, and new courage are gained. Those weary from ongoing battles find refuge from the everyday struggles of life and experience victorious strength.

A clear sense of His presence, the attributes of mercy and harmony, is worth faithful devotion. The eternal dividends from joining a covenant-community are substantive and priceless.

Community

A covenant-community has *divinely called leaders* and *devoted followers of Jesus*. When both are evident, grace and peace are abundantly seen. A bit of literary prose renders an important aspect of church.

It is composed of people just like me.
It will be friendly if I am.
It will do a great work if I work.
It will make generous gifts to many causes if I am generous.
It will bring others into fellowship if I bring them.
Its seats will be filled if I fill them.
It will be a church of loyalty and love, of faith and service,
If I, who make it what it is, am filled with these.
Therefore, with God's help, I give myself to the task of being,
All these things I want my church to be. (Author Unknown)

PRAYER

In the classic movie "Miss Congeniality," Sandra Bullock plays the role of an undercover federal agent participating in a beauty contest. Her tomboyish demeanor caused her to mock a worn-out response, frequently given by contestants. When asked what they wanted most, the standard reply was, "World peace!" In the final scene of the movie she is awarded the title Miss Congeniality and responds by saying weepily, "I really do want world peace."

Deep within the human soul, people are looking for peace, a peace only embedded in the fiber and fortitude of the church. Blessed peace is found in the Prince of Peace and cannot be witnessed among the nations until experienced in the human condition.

Jesus offers to everyone an incomprehensible peace, able to sustain a person in the worst of circumstances. To fully sense deep-seated peace involves Christ and the church.

Life in the Son implies a binding agreement, a covenant. The Heavenly Father gave a mutually beneficial promise, having His Son provide the signature in red. Will you place your pledge next to His? Will you decide to have faith in God and become included in the covenant-community. Your commitment involves the repentance of sin and the confession of His Lordship. Your signature is applied by praying a sincere petition. Allow Him to lead your life, join His heaven-bound community, and gain the satisfaction of an all-encompassing peace.

"Dear Lord, peace has escaped me for such a very long time. My heart desperately longs to experience Your perfect purpose for my life. I am convinced nothing in this world can provide the inner harmony I want and need. Please wash away the guilt and shame of my rebellious nature, often dominating my thoughts, feelings, and actions and hindering the heavenly tranquility craved in my soul. Lead and guide me in the way of truth and goodwill. Help me to fulfill Your custom-designed plan for my life with the abundance of life-guiding peace. Amen."

CHAPTER TWO

BLESSED

Blessed be the God and Father of our Lord Jesus Christ, who has blessed us in Christ with every spiritual blessing in the heavenly places, even as he chose us in him before the foundation of the world, that we should be holy and blameless before him. In love he predestined us for adoption as sons through Jesus Christ, according to the purpose of his will, to the praise of his glorious grace, with which he has blessed us in the Beloved. In him we have redemption through his blood, the forgiveness of our trespasses, according to the riches of his grace, which he lavished upon us, in all wisdom and insight making known to us the mystery of his will, according to his purpose, which he set forth in Christ as a plan for the fullness of time, to unite all things in him, things in heaven and things on earth. In him we have obtained an inheritance, having been predestined according to the purpose of him who works all things according to the counsel of his will, so that we who were the first to hope in Christ might be to the praise of his glory. In him you also, when you heard the word of truth, the gospel of your salvation, and believed in him, were sealed with the promised Holy Spirit, who is the guarantee of our inheritance until we acquire possession of it, to the praise of his glory. (Ephesians 1:3-14)

The church is a covenant-community and serves as the delivery system of God's story. The letter to the Ephesians helps people understand this unique gathering of Christ followers.

Years ago a phrase was introduced to describe life on this planet: "global village." With the advancement of communications and an increase of economic dependence among nations, the earth does seem much smaller. Some imagine this increases a sense of worldwide community. Actually, people feel more threatened.

Vulnerability is causing a greater desire for self-sufficiency, independence, and even isolation. Since countries can no longer self-exist, and large bodies of water are unable to protect nations from danger, people attempt to do so individually, hiding behind *individualism*. This ideology has become the new self-appointed ruler – and life is growing *lonelier*.

A newspaper article entitled, "Speak now or forever hold it in," addresses this problematic trend: "This just in: Men are still lonely…. They still don't tell each other anything. Nobody's talking…except in the usual brief, jocko, instantly forgotten boy-banter. 'Hey there, Larry, how you doing pal? How is everything, big guy? What's going on these days?' And then there'll be a quick tit-for-tat of non-news: bright and blissfully inconsequential, or at least not terribly revealing.

"Few men tell each other anything they may actually be deeply affected by, anything they may really be thinking or feeling. Lonely: walking and talking and driving around in a sort of mutually agreed upon vacuum. No real information. *No real community*. I wonder if it must not also be exhausting, pedaling so hard to keep up the vigorous, hale and hearty, everything's-fine façade?"

In earlier times followers of Jesus addressed each other as *brothers* or *sisters* in the Lord. Has a sense of family now become lost? The church designed as a covenant-community should be a place where men and women can put down an "everything's-fine façade."

Paul's letter begins by mentioning two critical components of a church, divinely called leaders and devoted followers of Jesus. Grace and peace are evident when both are present.

The next several lines are actually one extremely long sentence. They may have been a hymn, created and sung in the Early Church. Of the 36 times "in Christ" or its equivalent is found in this letter, ten occur in this section.

When reading these lines some people debate the subject of *chosen* and *predestined*. Did God choose only certain people to be saved? Did He predestine only some to experience salvation? Before looking at the actual focus of this part of the letter, consider the theological issue of election and predestination.

Do *election* and *predestination* refer to *people* being saved or the *plan* and *purpose* of salvation? The key phrase is "in Christ." God elected a salvation in which people abide *in Christ* and become holy and blameless in His sight. God purposed that every person abiding *in Christ* experiences abundant life.

Election is the *plan* of salvation, experienced *in Christ* through the atoning sacrifice of Mount Calvary. The election embraces *any* individual identifying and associating with Jesus. God elected to give salvation to *everyone* steadfast *in Him*. This salvation is experienced by *anyone* choosing to place faith *in Christ*.

Predestination refers to the *purposes* of God becoming fully experienced by everyone who enters the elected plan of salvation. God predestined those *in Christ* to be justified, conformed to His likeness, adopted as His children, recipients of the Holy Spirit, and created for goodness. Predestination refers to His *purposes* becoming complete in *every* individual abiding *in Christ*, the elected plan of salvation.

God elected to implement a *plan* of salvation involving everyone abiding *in Christ* and predestined His *purposes* being fully experienced through a new-found relationship *with Christ*.

With the ultimate plan of salvation as the backdrop,

what wonderful truth is Paul expressing to his friends? Simply this: God has *blessed* the covenant-community.

The promise

As God is Spirit, worshiped in spirit and truth (John 4:24), His blessings are *spiritual*. The blessing for the church is something intangible to those living for the visible and physical, something incomprehensible to anyone living only for the moment.

The spiritual blessing is also in *heavenly places*. Jesus said, "My kingdom is not of this world." (John 18:36) Only those entering His *heavenly* kingdom know of His *spiritual* blessings.

In the 70's and 80's, a lot of emphasis in the covenant-community was placed upon *material* blessings. Some influential leaders promoted living for Christ made a person a *King's kids*, and with enough faith, they could live in wealth and prosperity. Jesus has a far better plan; live in the indescribable blessings of His heavenly kingdom. Gain from His imperishable grace the wealth of eternity.

Jesus warned the church in Laodicea, "For you say, I am rich, I have prospered, and I need nothing, not realizing that you are wretched, pitiable, poor, blind, and naked. I counsel you to *buy from me* gold refined by fire, so that you may be rich, and white garments so that you may clothe yourself and the shame of your nakedness may not be seen, and salve to anoint your eyes, so that you may see." (Revelation 3:17-18)

The promise to the covenant-community is spiritual blessings in heavenly places.

The recipient

Recipients of spiritual blessings are to be pure and righteous. Anyone still living in rebellion toward God will not experience spiritual blessings. Insurrection and resurrection cannot coexist. Blessings are for those who walk and talk in grace.

"Holy" refers to *purity*, a life patterned after Jesus. When a person fully yields to the Holy Spirit, they begin to progressively conform into His image. The more *individualism* decreases and *Christ* increases, the more apparent are the spiritual blessings.

"Blameless" refers to being *without guilt*, living in a righteous manner where nothing must be hidden. The glimmer of grace exposes the darkness of defiance. Behavior is no longer shameful. Living guiltlessly brings transparency.

The benefits

Believers are rescued from evil. Jesus paid the necessary price and freed His followers from a rebellious nature, along with its consequences. Once they were captive to individualism but now are released from its grip, a great blessing.

Believers are forgiven. Thieves hope to hear the word, "Forgiven!" when standing before an angry employer or judge. They want the weight of embarrassment lifted from their heart. People can exist with meager earnings but not without peace of mind.

Lines are growing grayer between right and wrong yet feelings of shame, often deeply buried, still wrestle in the soul. In Christ comes the promise: "If we confess our sins, he is faithful and just and *will forgive* us our sins and purify us from all unrighteousness." (1 John 1:9)

Believers are adopted into the family of God. The relationship changes from Creator/created to Father/child.

Many people experience confusion about spiritual matters on account of poor parenting. They fail to grasp the promises of the Heavenly Father, mixing bewilderment with thoughts of blessings. Yet children raised in healthy families understand they hold a special place in the heart of their parents. Similarly, believers are radically loved by Jesus and abundantly blessed.

Believers gain an inheritance. They become a benefactor in His Last Will and Testament. What is inherited? "And he carried me away in the Spirit to a mountain great and high, and showed me the Holy City, Jerusalem, coming down out of heaven from God. It shone with the glory of God, and its brilliance was like that of a very precious jewel, like a jasper, clear as crystal…. The wall was made of jasper, and the city of pure gold, as pure as glass. The foundations of the city walls were decorated with every kind of precious stone…. The twelve gates were twelve pearls, each gate made of a single pearl. The great street of the city was of pure gold, like transparent glass.... Then the angel showed me the river of the water of life, as clear as crystal, flowing from the throne of God and of the Lamb down the middle of the great street of the city. On each side of the river stood the tree of life, bearing twelve crops of fruit, yielding its fruit every month. And the leaves of the tree are for the healing of the nations.... And I heard a loud voice from the throne saying, "Now the dwelling of God is with men, and he will live with them. They will be his people, and God himself will be with them and be their God. He will wipe every tear from their eyes. There will be no more death or mourning or crying or pain, for the old order of things has passed away." (Revelation 21:10-11, 18-19a, 21; 22:1-2; 21:3-4)

Believers are blessed with an immediate grace and a future hope.

The guarantee

A pledge or down payment has been posted, giving assurance of His blessing. The Holy Spirit has been deposited into the believer's eternal *bank account* and recorded on their spiritual *bank record*. His official seal is upon their heavenly *bank note*, binding the covenant. His presence within them is the evidence of blessing and His wonders flowing through them is the testimony.

If the coming of the Holy Spirit is only a down payment, greater dividends are coming. The average down payment for most major purchases is around ten or twenty percent of the full price. If the marvelous Holy Spirit is simply a deposit, the fullness of eternity must be majestic and immeasurable.

When believers gather, worship is usually expressed joyfully in voice and action. Yet eternity will manifest the full expression of jubilee. The excitement associated with present-day heavenly moments cannot match the enthusiasm of heavenly places.

The purpose

The blessing is "to the praise of His glory." Three times the phrase is mentioned, (Vs. 6, 12, 14) the first relating to the Father, the second to the Son, and the third to the Holy Spirit. The Triune God is the full expression of the spiritual blessings in heavenly places. Those following Jesus gladly rejoice and give praise for His goodness – rescued, freed, forgiven, adopted, and heir.

No amount of earthly wealth will persuade others of His eternal treasure. Peace of mind, freedom from guilt, and deep-seated joy are the markings of the heavenly kingdom. Mansions and limousines, as well as diamonds and furs, fade in comparison to the testimony of spiritual blessings in heavenly places.

Completely blessed

People never imagined Charles Dutton would achieve anything. He spent many years imprisoned for manslaughter but later became a successful Broadway star. When asked how he managed to make such a remarkable transition, he replied, "Unlike the other prisoners, I never decorated my cell." Dutton resolved never to regard his cell as home.

Those who follow Jesus gain much when they do not accommodate themselves to the confines of this world but long for heavenly places. (Hebrews 11:16) The believers' riches are found solely in spiritual blessings.

CHAPTER THREE

EXPECT

For this reason, because I have heard of your faith in the Lord Jesus and your love toward all the saints, I do not cease to give thanks for you, remembering you in my prayers, that the God of our Lord Jesus Christ, the Father of glory, may give you the Spirit of wisdom and of revelation in the knowledge of him, having the eyes of your hearts enlightened, that you may know what is the hope to which he has called you, what are the riches of his glorious inheritance in the saints, and what is the immeasurable greatness of his power toward us who believe, according to the working of his great might that he worked in Christ when he raised him from the dead and seated him at his right hand in the heavenly places, far above all rule and authority and power and dominion, and above every name that is named, not only in this age but also in the one to come. And he put all things under his feet and gave him as head over all things to the church, which is his body, the fullness of him who fills all in all.

(Ephesians 1:15-23)

The letter to the Ephesians shows the heavenly design of the church. A group of believers can choose to either be a *crowd* or a *community*. The primary focus of a *crowd* is events, leading to a roller coaster existence. Crowds are either emotionally up or down based on the effectiveness of activities. The primary focus of *community* is loving one another. *Relationships* are the best bedrock for sensing worth and finding meaning.

A loss of togetherness and brotherhood is growing exponentially throughout the world, including in the *United* States.

"Like a canoer paddling upstream, most Americans believe that they can go against the current while their country is being swept down the rivers of time. The majority of Americans see a radically different picture when they look into the future of their country and their own future. They believe that for America things are going to get worse, but for them life is going to get better. Only one in four of us thinks that America will be better off a year from now. But the majority believes that we ourselves will be better off – that what happens to America won't happen to us…. The great divide: Americans are disengaging their personal futures from our national destiny. Most Americans think that their own futures are going to be fine and dandy. They have become so alienated from the whole that they think they will be individually immune from the fate that they believe will befall the nation as a whole." (<u>The Day America Told the</u>

Truth, by James Patterson and Peter Kim)

What people think about society also reflects what believers believe about the church. Are you feeling you can disengage your personal spiritual life from the covenant-community and be just fine? You are wrong. God designed and initiated the church, and made her the instrument for preparing everyone for eternity.

Do you maintain a tidy backyard at your house; lawn well-manicured and groomed, the garden weed-free and carefully arranged? Has the garbage been placed in bins with the opening properly secured? Is everything in place and nothing out of order?

What about your neighbor? Do they have the same values? Imagine their lawn as full of crabgrass and unkempt, their garden choked with weeds and thistles, and debris scattered everywhere. Picture rats making a home in your neighbor's junk piles, the barbecue grill caked with old grease and burnt meat, and old picnic fixings sitting on the table. Daily you see various insects swarming everywhere.

Under such conditions, is your child able to play happily in your beautiful backyard? No doubt, you would leap to action if, looking out the kitchen window, you saw flies teeming around your child and rats invading your garden.

Even though you maintained a tidy little yard, your property cannot be detached from the unkempt property of a neighbor. Similarly, what happens in church impacts every follower of Jesus, whether they participate vigorously or sporadically!

Disengaging from others in Christ is morally wrong, violating love of neighbor. Criticism, cynicism, blame, accusation, and slander are growing within the ranks of believers; all signs of disconnected people.

Without close ties, flaws are more readily seen instead of the finer qualities. A covenant-community is designed to build-up, encourage, appreciate, and compliment; attributes demonstrating faith.

Paul expresses two prayers in this letter. He had been hearing wonderful reports about the church and mentions in the first prayer two areas where they were excelling; they believed God for great things and had a genuine affection for one another. They had an active type of faith and love. Instead of ruled by circumstances, they were patterning their lives according to the will of God. They sincerely wanted the Lord to be glorified through them.

All of Paul's prayers are ageless. They are for every church where faith and love are active. As a result of his earnest petition, what should followers of Jesus in every generation expect until Christ returns?

Wisdom and revelation

Paul writes about the "Spirit of wisdom and revelation." He prayed for the Holy Spirit to give believers a greater awareness of the one True God. The Spirit helps followers of Jesus to realize His participation in every circumstance.

The Spirit of *wisdom* is more than judgment and intuition derived from human reasoning. Rather, it is heaven-sent wisdom, supernatural understanding, and correct judgment about the true nature of God. Misconceptions are cleared up when divine wisdom is present. Followers of Jesus have the ability to genuinely know "the Father of glory."

The Spirit of *revelation* is the *unveiling* or *uncovering* of the will of God, knowledge beyond ordinary means. The revelation is not a mysterious and mystical unveiling of the unknown but an energizing uncovering of truth.

Charlatans have adulterated the term *revelation*. Egocentric revelations have caused within the covenant-community such things as divisiveness, grief, anguish, heartache, contention, and ruin. Every good gift of God can be selfishly abused. Rather than reject everything associated with the concept of revelation, intensify a desire to experience holy discernment.

A.W. Tozer observed: "The teaching of the New Testament is that God and spiritual things can be known fully only by a direct work of God within the soul. Theological knowledge may be aided by figures and analogies, however, the pure understanding of God must be by personal spiritual awareness. The Holy Spirit is indispensable."

Expect the Spirit of wisdom and revelation to aid

your knowledge of God, increasing your ability to accomplish His mission.

An enlightened heart

The early church "kept *feeling* a sense of awe." (Acts 2:43) Becoming *awestruck* only comes from an enlightened heart. The Holy Spirit wants to turn on a heavenly light bulb deep within, illuminating and enriching the inward nature.

Is your *heart* actively pursuing God – intellect, emotion, and will? An enlightened heart weakens the persuasive power of public opinion and the influence of errant conclusions. Worldly pressure loses potency with an awakened heart and loses the ability to unsaddle faith in Jesus, as well as a love for others.

The combination of *knowing, feeling* and *doing* gives an enhanced alertness to His glory. The Lord should be known reasonably, yet avoid having only an intellectual awareness. Comprehend from the heart, the mainstay of life, the fullness of God.

Greater perception

With the Spirit of wisdom and revelation and with an enlightened heart, three truths become embraced more fully.

The hope of His calling. Hope refers to an expectant attitude. A sense of anticipation saturates the soul. Hope in God, contrary to a mere natural hope, changes personal perceptions from *wish* to *know*. The hope of His calling gives a special assurance that God will consummate all the promises He has given to the covenant-community.

Secondly, *the riches of His glorious inheritance*. The full majesty of heaven and eternity with God comes to light. The beauty of a rain forest, the magnificence of mountains, the wonder of oceans, the fragrance of tropical islands cannot compare to the richness of God's kingdom.

Pure gold covers the roads of the Celestial City. When compared to the splendor of heaven, is the brilliance of gold nothing more than the drabness of asphalt? The wealthy of this world often think poorly of followers of Jesus, yet believers are rich in eternal value.

Thirdly, *His incomparably great power*. Four different terms for potency are contained in the prayer. *Power* gives attention to capability. *Working* addresses operative power. *Strength* deals with manifest power. *Might* focuses on possessive power. Paul is conveying, "His incomparably great [capability] for us who believe... is like the [operative power] of the [manifested power] of His [possessive power]." (V. 19) The supreme capacity of God was fully demonstrated by the resurrection of Jesus from the dead, the glory of life-giving power.

With the Spirit of wisdom and revelation and with an enlightened heart, those following Christ can reap His infinite hope, realize His endless riches, and experience His unlimited power.

Expect

Seek the Spirit of wisdom and revelation, pursue an enlightened heart, and abide in holy wonder. Gain greater hope and rely on overcoming power!

Herbert Jackson as a new missionary was assigned a car that would not start without a push. After pondering his problem, he devised a plan. He went to the school near his home, got permission to take some children out of class and had them push his car. As he made his rounds he would either park on a hill or leave his car running. He used this ingenious procedure for two years.

Ill health forced the Jackson family to leave and a new missionary came to take his place. When Herbert proudly began to explain his arrangement for getting the car started the new missionary began looking under the hood. Before the explanation was complete the person interrupted, "Dr. Jackson the only trouble is this loose cable on the starter motor." Giving the cable a twist, stepping into the car, turning the switch, the engine roared to life to Jackson's astonishment. For two years, needless trouble had become routine. The power was there all the time. Only a loose connection kept Jackson from putting power to work.

The power available to those with faith in God is tremendous! When your connection with God is firm, His life and power flow freely. Holy Spirit wisdom and revelation combined with an enlightened heart bring hope and power into your situation.

Personalize the prayer that Paul prayed for *you*! Expect his prayer to be answered in Christ.

S. ROBERT MADDOX

CHAPTER FOUR

BELOVED

And you were dead in the trespasses and sins in which you once walked, following the course of this world, following the prince of the power of the air, the spirit that is now at work in the sons of disobedience—among whom we all once lived in the passions of our flesh, carrying out the desires of the body and the mind, and were by nature children of wrath, like the rest of mankind. But God, being rich in mercy, because of the great love with which he loved us, even when we were dead in our trespasses, made us alive together with Christ—by grace you have been saved—and raised us up with him and seated us with him in the heavenly places in Christ Jesus, so that in the coming ages he might show the immeasurable riches of his grace in kindness toward us in Christ Jesus. For by grace you have been saved through faith. And this is not your own doing; it is the gift of God, not a result of works, so that no one may boast. For we are his workmanship, created in Christ Jesus for good works, which God prepared beforehand, that we should walk in them. (Ephesians 2:1-10)

I once read an article entitled, "Moving from Solitude, to Community, to Ministry," emphasizing a relationship with God begins with solitude, a place where a person can hear God relating to them as *beloved.* In these moments of intimate *communion,* the *call* of *community* is detected, the cherished gathering of the beloved children of God.

Why is the order of solitude preceding community important? If believers do not comprehend they are God's beloved, they expect those within the community to make them feel beloved. They expect a *person* to give them perfect love, which no one can do.

Love coming from the fallen nature is imperfect and contains stipulations, such as "I'll love you as long as you meet my expectations … I'll love you as long as you do what I want … I'll love you as long as you think like me … I'll love you as long as I get my way." Less than perfect people cannot adequately address the need of unconditional and absolute acceptance.

Followers of Jesus are to blend solitude with community. The result? The church becomes the *beloved* rejoicing with the *beloved,* instead of the *lonely* finding solace with the *lonely.* When every believer is experiencing love from the same source, namely the Heavenly Father, then the correctly formulated *Church of the Beloved* is witnessed.

What can someone expect from the Church of the Beloved? A covenant-community sincerely expressing forgiveness and celebration! The most forgiving people on the face of the earth are devoted followers of Jesus, but they are not gullible. Forgiveness involves confession, repentance, godly sorrow, and genuine remorse.

Forgiveness is allowing the other person *to not be God*. Forgiveness says, "I love you not because you are perfect but because you are beloved." When followers of Jesus gather in merciful and undemanding ways, liberation comes into their gathering.

In the instructions for healing given by James is attached the phrase, "Therefore confess your sins to each other and pray for each other so that you may be healed." (James 5:16) Healing is manifested in vulnerability and weakness. In the Church of the Beloved, a person should be able to admit "I have flaws" and still find acceptance.

Society rarely allows this. No one dares risk showing weaknesses in a dog-eat-dog world. In my opinion, people should view with sincere sympathy public officials and various celebrities. Regardless of their errant outlooks or misguided conduct, unless they hide their flaws the media is unmerciful. The average news reporter could not stand up to the scrutiny they put famous people through and they know no such expectations are demanded of their actions. Investigative reporting usually ends up a witch hunt.

In the Biblical narrative of Noah is an unpleasant

story about him becoming intoxicated and exposing himself. (Genesis 9:20-23) Yet the event shows the acceptable conduct of his family without condoning his appalling behavior. Two sons covered the shamefulness of their beloved father.

Peter instructs the church family, "Above all, love each other deeply, because love covers over a multitude of sins." (1 Peter 4:8) By everyone gaining their sense of worth from the Heavenly Father, the beloved community is liberated to lovingly forgive. (Galatians 6:1-2)

The church is a covenant-community. Each believer demonstrates their covenant with God by joining ranks with others who love Him and then collectively serve Him. How does Paul describe those in the Church of the Beloved?

Completely fallen

"And you were dead…." (V.1) Because of a world innately rebellious and willfully defiant, tangible physical death reigns. Yet, though presently alive, people without Christ are already spiritually dead. Out of the full realm of transgressions (*trespasses* and *sins*), no one can fulfill the original design of creation.

The word *trespass* conveys the idea of *blunder* or *mistake*, things associated with an *errant* nature. The word *sin* carries the concept of *want* or *choice*, things associated with an *unruly* nature. Whether unintentional or intentional, the result is the same; deadness.

Three forces work against someone following and reflecting Jesus. *The course of the world*; the sleazy environment influencing people by *seduction*. (V.2) *The prince of the power of the air*; the evil one influencing people by *deception*. (V.2) *The spirit of disobedience*; the inner corruption influencing people by *temptation*. (V.3)

The *seduction of worldliness* is seen in a story about a home overrun by mice. The owner bought several D-Con boxes and distributed them around the house, including under the bed. During the night, the mice were heard in a feeding frenzy. In the morning, the boxes were checked and licked clean. To make sure they were all gone more boxes were set out the next night. The mice went for the poison like piranha. In the days that followed all was quiet. The ways of this world may be popular and appetizing but they are deadly.

The *deception of Satan* is described in the story of Jose Cubero, one of Spain's most brilliant matadors. By his 21st birthday, he was already enjoying a spectacular career. Yet in his last bullfight, he made a tragic mistake. He thrust his sword a final time into a bleeding delirious bull that then collapsed. Considering the struggle completed he turned to the crowd but the bull was not dead. The animal rose and lunged at the unsuspecting matador. A horn pierced his back and punctured his heart. Just when you think the devil is *dead* he rises up and pierces from behind.

The *temptation of corruption* is best summed up in a magazine cartoon. Jesus is depicted as saying, "If I'm OK and you're OK, what am I doing hanging on a cross?" No one is okay, everyone needs a Savior.

Jesus manifested natural *desires* in a righteous sense, "He said to them, 'I have earnestly desired to eat this Passover with you before I suffer.'" (Luke 22:15) Paul highlights natural *desires* in a wicked sense, "…indulging the desires of the flesh and of the mind." (V. 3) When desires come from the *spiritual* nature, the results are decent. When desires come from the *sinful* nature, the outcome is depravity. The very ambition driving you can also defeat you. Recognize the source of your desires.

Paul concisely communicates that those in Christ were once spiritually dead. (Vs. 1-3) They had nothing pleasant to anticipate. There was no hope for a better future.

Completely raised up

After carefully showing total spiritual deadness, the grammatical conjunction "but God" follows close behind, meaning, *however, on the other hand, or nevertheless*. The Lord has provided the perfect remedy. Heavenly love has been activated. Divine mercy was triggered in Christ.

While dead in transgressions *God made believers alive*. He implanted *eternal life* where *spiritual deadness* once existed.

While dead in transgressions *God raised believers up*. They are raised to a new life in Christ. The aliveness is discovered by following Jesus. No one can raise themselves from spiritual deadness nor bring themselves to eternal life. The merciful God performs the supernatural experience.

Having been once dead in transgressions, *God has seated believers in heavenly places*. Paul highlights a glorious progression. The church is blessed with spiritual blessings "in heavenly places." (1:3) Jesus was raised and is seated "in heavenly places." (1:20) And those in Christ have been raised and are seated "in heavenly places." (2:6)

Having such a wonderful blessing, then why are believers bogged down with earthly concerns? Career aspirations are relevant but not to the hindrance of spiritual aliveness. Professional achievements are noble yet insignificant in light of heavenly places. God has created people for higher and nobler endeavors.

The Church was once accused of being so *heavenly-minded*, she was no earthly good. Has the Church now become so *earthly-minded*, she is no heavenly good? Those who follow Jesus are the beloved, the church is the beloved community, and God has risen up the beloved to experience lofty blessings.

Completely undeserved

"By grace you have been saved." (V. 8) *Grace*, undeserved favor, explains the spiritual operation. No act of God is done toward anyone because they deserve or earn it. No one merits becoming eternally alive. By nature (trespasses) and by choice (sins) believers were once rebellious and disobedient. God simply decided out of genuine love to be kind.

Grace is the *basis* of salvation. Yet living in a task-oriented world causes some to attempt salvation by *working good deeds* and others by *working up faith*. Neither is the correct approach.

Many try to achieve a *mustered-up faith*. They try to continually think positively and refuse to view life with realism. Blind and cheerful optimism cannot produce solutions, nor salvation.

Jesus, however, highlights *mustard-seed faith*. (Luke 17:6) People are to rely on the *measure of faith* (Romans 12:2), already given by God, and accept His undeserved gift. Divine grace *gives* salvation and people must, by faith, simply say yes to His provision.

Beware of Pharisaic faith, a personal prideful faith. Salvation is not self-achieved by doing good deeds nor by developing unwarranted optimism.

Completely fallen, completely raised, completely undeserved!

A work of art

Paul ends his comments by mentioning God's workmanship. In Christ, believers are a work of art; His masterpiece. As a product of divine craftsmanship, they are to reflect by actions and attitudes His astounding artistry. Conduct is associated with following Jesus, not entering salvation.

Hudson Taylor said, "I used to ask God to help me. Then I asked if I might help him. I ended up asking him to do his work through me." Well said!

What does your life reveal about you? What role do righteous qualities play in your life? Does your behavior show His masterpiece? Good conduct will not bring grace; rather, it is the outgrowth of living a life of trust. By becoming spiritually alive in Christ, *ambition* reverts to *abiding* in the robe of Christ's righteousness.

The Church of the Beloved

If honest and sincere caring for *one another* does not occur in the local church, people search for this need to be addressed elsewhere. Everyone naturally seeks to belong to some type of satisfying cause, whether the purpose is for good or evil, builds or destroys. Service organizations, fitness centers, sports clubs, and even the occult are increasingly becoming substitutes for virtuous values.

A clean and spotless sense of community is quickly vanishing throughout the world. Unfortunately, followers of Jesus are equally downplaying the importance of these attributes in the covenant-community. Believers must initiate a restoration of righteousness in the Church of the Beloved that will spill onto the nations.

Embrace the call to be the Church of the Beloved, the source of authentic community, the place of unmerited acceptance, and the model of moral decency.

CHAPTER FIVE

DESIGN

Therefore remember that at one time you Gentiles in the flesh, called "the uncircumcision" by what is called the circumcision, which is made in the flesh by hands— remember that you were at that time separated from Christ, alienated from the commonwealth of Israel and strangers to the covenants of promise, having no hope and without God in the world. But now in Christ Jesus you who once were far off have been brought near by the blood of Christ. For he himself is our peace, who has made us both one and has broken down in his flesh the dividing wall of hostility by abolishing the law of commandments expressed in ordinances, that he might create in himself one new man in place of the two, so making peace, and might reconcile us both to God in one body through the cross, thereby killing the hostility. And he came and preached peace to you who were far off and peace to those who were near. For through him we both have access in one Spirit to the Father. So then you are no longer strangers and aliens, but you are fellow citizens with the saints and members of the household of God, built on the foundation of the apostles and prophets, Christ Jesus himself being the cornerstone, in whom the whole structure, being joined together, grows into a holy temple in the Lord. In him you also are being built together into a dwelling place for God by the Spirit. (Ephesians 2:11-22)

Paul's letter teaches about the covenant-community. As a sense of community deteriorates in America, how is this affecting the church?

Linda Burkhard served as the principle of the Olive Mary Stitt Elementary School in the Chicago area. She regularly sent newsletters to parents called the "Olive Branch." One of her letters made the following comments: "Neighborhood socializing has declined over the past two decades. The proportion of Americans saying people can be trusted fell by more than a third in the last 30 years. There has been a 25% decline in the turnout of people for national elections since a highpoint that occurred in the 60's. Since 1973, the number of Americans who reported attending in the past year a public, school or town meeting, served on a committee or local organization, or worked for a political party has dropped by more than a third. Volunteers for the Red Cross is down 61% since 1970. Traditional forms of involvement have declined, new organizations have gained members, but they are different – involvement is simply writing a check or reading a newsletter. These groups are different in that bonding together for networking, for support, for trusting relationships, and for mutual goals are not required."

Robert Putman, from Harvard University, wrote in *Bowling Alone: America's Declining Social Capital* why social hubs are eroding. The main reasons include wives and husbands both active in the labor force, which means less time for building social centers; increased mobility of families, which reduces civic engagement; demographic changes such as fewer marriages, more divorces and fewer children; and technological transformation of leisure, which focuses more on individual recreation, creating a loss of positive social group activities and collective interest.

What do the observations of Burkhard and Putman have in common? They are describing the same thing. Society is losing community, which leads to anarchy. Individualism always ushers in rebellion, with everyone doing what is right in their own eyes (Judges 17-21).

Alexander Tytler describes a major weakness in the ancient Athenian model of democracy, something equally relevant today: "A democracy cannot exist as a permanent form of government. It can only exist until the voters discover that they can vote themselves money from the Public Treasury. From that moment on the majority always votes for candidates promising the most benefits from the Public Treasury...with the result that a democracy always collapses over loose fiscal policy, always followed by a dictatorship. The average of the world's greatest civilizations has been 200 years. These nations have progressed through the following sequence: From bondage to spiritual faith, from spiritual faith to great courage, from courage to liberty, from liberty to abundance, from abundance to selfishness, from selfishness to complacency, from complacency to apathy, from apathy to dependence, from dependence back into bondage."

Where is the global community currently in this pattern? Does the universal de-emphasizing of *togetherness* also affect those endeavoring to live for Jesus? Like cultural individualism, spiritual individualism erodes the covenant-community. The genuine Church of the Beloved, the divine plan for community, is the model the world desperately needs to see.

Wherever there are people, there is the potential for division. Paul wrote about the division surrounding the rite of circumcision. Circumcision was instituted as an external sign of the covenant made with Abraham (Genesis 17:10-14) but the custom eventually became a barrier between Jew and Gentile, having little to do with an association with God. Contempt went both ways, Gentiles toward Jews and Jews toward Gentiles. Something intended for good became an obstacle.

How does a problem like this become solved? How can a pure sense of community become restored? Three approaches are often attempted: A committee is created to study the issue, an arbitration board is created to resolve the matter, or a pluralistic approach is taken that seeks tolerance and understanding by all concerned parties.

God chose a better way. He made everyone the same *body* and built a *temple* dedicated to bringing purpose to human existence. Community and personal value are accomplished through extraordinary instead of ordinary means.

Designed as a body

The church is more than an organization; she is a living organism. She breathes the breath of the Holy Spirit. Her heart beats the blood spilled on Golgotha. Her actions are directed by the control center, Jesus.

The church is abiding in the grace of the Heavenly Father and living like Christ under the guidance of the Holy Spirit. The eternal three-in-one God is working a holy transformation of His children.

How do you explain to business leaders how a church functions? She is more than a corporation run by executives. She is a living, pulsating, breathing organism birthed by God.

As a Body, the church can be healthy and full of vigor. She is strong when properly nourished, when every part is functioning normally, and when she maintains a proper balance between rest, diet, and exercise. She feels good by the *joy of the Lord*. Her complexion is radiant with the *peace of Christ*. She moves gracefully by the *unity of the Spirit*. She is a beautiful sight to behold when healthy and in top form.

As a Body, the church can become diseased and

terminal. She can become clammy and cold by the discord of her various members.

The Fable of the Belly shows the tragedy of discord: "One day it occurred to the members of the body that they were doing all the work and the belly was getting all the food. They held a meeting and called for a strike until the belly did its proper share of work. The hands refused to take food, the mouth refused to receive it, and the teeth had nothing to do. Soon the members of the body found themselves in a very non-active condition. Hands could hardly move, the mouth was parched and dry, and the legs were unable to support the physical frame. The belly in its dull quiet way was doing necessary work. Everything must function together or the body goes to pieces."

The church becomes sluggish by malnutrition, living on the spiritual junk food of distorted truth. She loses her mobility by bitterness. She misplaces her purpose when no longer breathing in the Holy Spirit: "Do not quench the Spirit." (1 Thessalonians 5:19) A church can commit these actions and quit receiving the life-giving energy of God.

The church is described as a body in First Corinthians: "For just as the body is one and has many members, and all the members of the body, though many, are one body, so it is with Christ. For in one Spirit we were all baptized into one body—Jews or Greeks, slaves or free—and all were made to drink of one Spirit. For the body does not consist of one member but of many. If the foot should say, 'Because I am not a hand, I do not belong to the body,' that would not make it any less a part of the body. And if the ear should say, 'Because I am not an eye, I do not belong to the body,' that would not make it any less a part of the body. If the whole body were an eye, where would be the sense of hearing? If the whole body were an ear, where would be the sense of smell? But as it is, God arranged the members in the body, each one of them, as he chose. If all were a single member, where would the body be? As it is, there are many parts, yet one body. The eye cannot say to the hand, 'I have no need of you,' nor again the head to the feet, 'I have no need of you.' ... Now you are the body of Christ and individually members of it." (1 Corinthians 12:12-21, 27)

God designed the church as a living, breathing organism.

Designed as a temple

The church is also a holy place, a place where God dwells. She is a place of *worship* to the one True God. She is a place of *adoration* to the kind and loving God. She is a place of *consecration*, where spiritual sandals are removed and a person's life is exposed to the burning bush of truth. She is called to live in *humbleness* and *meekness*. She is challenged to live in *submission* and *modesty*. In this temple, people appear before the Almighty.

As a temple, she is skillfully built. The *foundation* is the Apostles and Prophets who form the basis for faith and experience.

The *Cornerstone* is the Lord Jesus. The chief stone is placed at the main corner and binds together the structure. The stability of the temple depends on Him. The Cornerstone provides the standard for straight lines, both horizontally and vertically.

The church is built well when her purpose is honoring God and Him alone. Truth and honesty, in word and deed, builds His holy place.

As a temple, she can crack and crumble. She can *falter* by the puffing up of pride and the tickling ear of distortion. She can *corrode* by unclean hearts and impure motives. She can *wear away* by hypocrisy and spiritual arrogance. She can *teeter* by self-aggrandizement, usurping the throne of God.

This temple is the house of the living God. Her pillars and supports are called *truth*. Anything other than truth causes her to crack and crumble.

Church

God designed the church as a Body and a Temple. She is alive and holy; she can be healthy or diseased, well-built or crumbling.

Only in the church can division points between people be removed. Believers are no longer *far off* but *brought near* through Jesus. People are no longer *aliens*, no longer *strangers*, no longer *without hope,* because they are no longer *without God*.

Everyone belongs, everyone has a part, and everyone worships the one True God. The church is not *us and them,* but rather, *we!* Jesus is *our* peace. In short, she is the *covenant-community.*

As a Body of believers and a Temple of truth, the church addresses the need expressed in this prose:

If this is not a place where tears are understood,
Then where shall I go to cry?
And if this is not a place where my spirit can take wings,
Then where shall I go to fly?

I don't need another place for tryin' to impress you
With just how good and virtuous I am, no, no, no.
I don't need another place for always being on top of things.
Everybody knows that it's a sham, it's a sham.

I don't need another place for always wearin' smiles
Even when it's not the way I feel.
I don't need another place to mouth the same platitudes
Everybody knows that it's not real.

So if this is not a place where my questions can be asked,
Then where shall I go to seek?
And if this is not a place where my heart cry can be heard,
Where, tell me where, shall I go to speak?

So if this is not a place where tears are understood,
Where shall I go, where shall I go to fly?
(Author Unknown)

S. ROBERT MADDOX

CHAPTER SIX

MYSTERY

For this reason I, Paul, a prisoner for Christ Jesus on behalf of you Gentiles—assuming that you have heard of the stewardship of God's grace that was given to me for you, how the mystery was made known to me by revelation, as I have written briefly. When you read this, you can perceive my insight into the mystery of Christ, which was not made known to the sons of men in other generations as it has now been revealed to his holy apostles and prophets by the Spirit. This mystery is that the Gentiles are fellow heirs, members of the same body, and partakers of the promise in Christ Jesus through the gospel. Of this gospel I was made a minister according to the gift of God's grace, which was given me by the working of his power. To me, though I am the very least of all the saints, this grace was given, to preach to the Gentiles the unsearchable riches of Christ, and to bring to light for everyone what is the plan of the mystery hidden for ages in God who created all things, so that through the church the manifold wisdom of God might now be made known to the rulers and authorities in the heavenly places. This was according to the eternal purpose that he has realized in Christ Jesus our Lord, in whom we have boldness and access with confidence through our faith in him. So I ask you not to lose heart over what I am suffering for you, which is your glory. (Ephesians 3:1-13)

The church is a covenant-community comprised of divinely called leaders and devoted followers of Jesus, blessed by God with spiritual blessings, guided by heavenly wisdom and revelation, and highlights forgiveness and celebration. The church is designed as a living organism and a holy dwelling place. Therefore, a longstanding mystery is now able to finally be cleared up.

Good mysteries are always enjoyable to read. As a child, I read the Hardy Boys Mysteries. Today, I continue to be entertained by reading and watching mysteries. I find pleasure solving whodunits before they are disclosed.

Anyone loving mysteries should love the Bible. The New Testament contains the mystery of godliness, faith, the Kingdom, and the Second Coming. Christ dwelling within a person is one of the greatest mysteries of all.

Paul uses the word *mystery* 21 times in his writings. He is not referring to something mystical but, rather, revealing something once incomprehensible. Some secrets are kept so close to the heart of God that even heavenly beings, described as rulers and authorities in the heavenly places, are yet to understand. One mystery hidden for centuries from clear view has to do with restoring the *oneness* lost at the Tower of Babel. In Christ, being of *one heart and mind* has been redeemed.

"So Peter opened his mouth and said: 'Truly I understand that God shows no partiality....'" (Acts 10:34)

"There is neither Jew nor Greek, there is neither slave nor free, there is no male and female, for you are all one in Christ Jesus." (Galatians 3:28)

"For God shows no partiality." (Romans 2:11)

Originally, Gentiles could become Jewish proselytes and share in God's blessings, but a distinction always existed between them and those of Jewish birth. This is no longer the case in the covenant-community. People closely connected to God in Christ are *heirs together* in the family of faith, *members together* in the Church of the Beloved, and *sharers together* in the heavenly promises. (V. 6)

What human government cannot do, God did

Everyone is linked to the same ancestor, Adam. From Adam came Noah, from Noah came three sons, and from these three sons came all the people groups of the world. Initially, the human race spoke the same language. With the diversity of languages came other distinctions, additional division points.

Because of different languages, some are considered inferior. Doing well in any nation requires speaking the dominant language. A person quickly experiences disadvantages if unable to comprehend or speak the local dialect. In the global economy, English reigns as the language of travel and universal trade.

Because of different skin pigmentations, some are thought inferior. The problem is not limited to just North America. If not the majority skin color of a nation or region, a person is a minority. Yet life is in the blood, not the skin. The same blood flows through every human. Skin tone is an incidental issue.

Because of different physical features, some are believed inferior. My initial training in the Air Force was at Lackland AFB in San Antonio, Texas. New recruits immediately had their heads shaved and were required to be without hair the entire six-week period.

After Basic Training came Technical School at Lowery AFB, near Denver, Colorado. Airmen were housed in old WWII open-bay barracks, heated by coal-burning furnaces. New arrivals were referred to as "beeps," the make-believe sound of hair growing back. Minus hair, newcomers were thought inferior.

The second-floor residence had been on Base a few months longer than the first floor. One night, some upper floor Airmen decided to do a surprise attack, a "blanket party" on the main floor. The invaders were massacred. One Airman fleeing back upstairs was heard saying to his friend, "Man, for a bunch of *beeps* they sure are strong." Hair has not been a strength issue since Samson.

Because of different financial standings, some are deemed inferior. My father was a railroad engineer who happened to live in a wealthier part of Seattle. My grandparents moved to Magnolia Bluff before the area became preferred and prestigious.

My neighborhood friends had many privileges not experienced by my immediate family – regular trips to exotic places, new cars on their 16th birthdays, a fully-funded college education. The environment could easily have caused a railroad engineer's son to acquire a sense of inferiority, generating envy and resentment. Fortunately, those feelings never developed.

Because of different educational rankings, some are judged inferior. Academic standings mean everything in institutions of higher education. Faculty on college campuses are measured by advanced *degrees*. Yet in every other career, people are gauged by job *results*. A cursory glance of life reveals some academicians are needlessly puffed up and proud, perceiving themselves wise without measurable achievements in the very fields they attempt to teach.

The Good News announces the abolishment of every form of inferiority in Christ.

The church is about equality

Even though people are not identical in the covenant-community, they are equal. In Christ, everyone is communally under submission to God.

Whether a person *owns* a business or is *employed* by one, they are equal in Christ. Paul instructs the church, "Masters, treat your bondservants justly and fairly, knowing that you also have a Master in heaven." (Colossians 4:1) He also wrote his friend Philemon about his runaway slave Onesimus. The servant decided to follow Jesus and was now a brother and partner in Christ.

Men and *women* are equal in the church and in their access to the Heavenly Father. Faith in Jesus has done more to elevate the role of womanhood throughout the world than any other belief system.

Luke makes reference to the commonality found in Christ: "And all who believed were together and had all things in common." (Acts 2:44) "There was not a needy person among them … [*supplies were*] distributed to each as any had need." (Acts 4:34-35)

Paul shows throughout his writings various dimensions of equality: such as, if one hurts, all hurt; if one rejoices, all rejoice; if one has needs, all have a need. What happens to one follower of Jesus impacts the whole group of believers.

In nationality, gender, social status, educational rankings, and financial standings, everyone is commonly in Christ.

Some Jewish followers in the early church wanted new converts to include in their devotion to God the act of circumcision as well as adherence to the strict letter of the Law. Centuries later, various foreign missionaries attempted to westernize people more than reveal Jesus. Paul shows all needless confusion must stop. Faith in God transcends cultural demands and practices.

I was raised in a home with diverse political opinions. Politics proved to be inconsequential toward our relationship with one another because we were family. The covenant-community works best the exact same way.

Whether people are man or woman, possess dissimilar skin tones, speak different languages, vote liberal or conservative, everyone in Christ is equal.

The church administrates equality

Civil government cannot create equality but simply recognize all are created equal. The church also does not create but only upholds and honors the divinely-given blessing.

If not careful, people can easily slip into old patterns. "My brothers, show no partiality as you hold the faith in our Lord Jesus Christ, the Lord of glory. For if a man wearing a gold ring and fine clothing comes into your assembly, and a poor man in shabby clothing also comes in, and if you pay attention to the one who wears the fine clothing and say, 'You sit here in a good place,' while you say to the poor man, 'You stand over there,' or, 'Sit down at my feet,' have you not then made distinctions among yourselves and become judges with evil thoughts? Listen, my beloved brothers, has not God chosen those who are poor in the world to be rich in faith and heirs of the kingdom, which he has promised to those who love him?

… But if you show partiality, you are committing sin and are convicted by the law as transgressors." (James 2:1-5, 9)

James was giving attention to an issue *already happening* in the church. He was not trying to *prevent* but seeking to *stop* partiality. As administrators of equality, believers are to show the holy bond of commonality.

Regardless of the Declaration of Independence's Preamble, the United States is not the best model of equality to the world. Only the covenant-community has the means to be the clear beacon of oneness.

Is the church revealing the mystery of equality? While overseeing a congregation in a small Minnesota town, only a few local ministers emphasized the importance of being *born from above*. Three of these pastors worked harmoniously to fervently accentuate this life-changing decision. Yet another minister, who communicated the same message, would have nothing to do with anyone failing to embrace all the doctrines of his church affiliation. Even a minister, whose denomination was closely connected to his, failed the litmus test.

The town also had various branches of the Lutheran church. One minister would not participate in the monthly gatherings of local clergy. The reason? His offshoot would not allow ministers to pray with non-Lutherans.

Many Christian groups have allowed petty distinctions to send a confusing message to the unchurched. Am I Pentecostal in belief? Positively! Do I publicly declare the baptism in the Holy Spirit accompanied with an evidential sign? Absolutely! Do I disassociate from those refusing to acknowledge this experience? No! A person's standing with God is solely connected to the death and resurrection of Jesus.

Mystery solved

In the covenant-community is equality. All things are held in common among the followers of Jesus. Everyone is uniformly under submission to God. Partiality and favoritism are horrendous errors. In Christ, every kind of barrier has been completely torn down.

CHAPTER SEVEN

FULLNESS

For this reason I bow my knees before the Father, from whom every family in heaven and on earth is named, that according to the riches of his glory he may grant you to be strengthened with power through his Spirit in your inner being, so that Christ may dwell in your hearts through faith—that you, being rooted and grounded in love, may have strength to comprehend with all the saints what is the breadth and length and height and depth, and to know the love of Christ that surpasses knowledge, that you may be filled with all the fullness of God. (Ephesians 3:14-19)

A mystery has been cleared up. Everyone is equal in Christ. Whether a person is a man or woman, blond or brunette, plain or pretty, tall or short, large or small, dark or light skin, awkward or eloquent, liberal or conservative, well-off or destitute, the ground around the cross of Calvary is perfectly level.

Paul now expresses a second prayer for his friends. He once again talks to God on behalf of those in Christ.

Just before praying he writes, "For this reason...." The same phrase was first seen at the beginning of the chapter. Was he sidetracked for a moment and now returning to an earlier train-of-thought?

"For this reason," and then prays. What reason? The world has collapsed into chaos. Strife is increasing amid *nations*, *neighbors* and the *nucleus* of the soul. The conflict is creating division among groups, between friends, and within the inward nature. Every form of anarchy can be brought into harmony in Christ.

Paul prays for believers to experience the source of synchronization: "That you may be *filled* with all the *fullness* of God." (V.19) Abundance is involved, coming from the Father, Son, and Holy Spirit. Each person of the Holy Trinity contributes to the *solution*, ushering in a sense of completeness. What should a believer expect on account of this prayer?

From the Father: Glory (V.16)

The richness of divine glory is a main topic of Scripture. An event in the life of Moses provides a functional understanding of His majesty.

When Israel set up camp in the wilderness, Moses erected the Tent of Meeting. By entering the sacred place, a cloud would descend and the Lord would speak to Moses "as a man speaks to a friend." (Exodus 33:11)

The Psalmist revealed, "He made known his ways to Moses, his acts to the people of Israel. (Psalm 103:7) Moses was learning God's *ways* in the Tent of Meeting and the people, witnessing the cloud, were seeing His *acts*. Knowing His ways is much more enriching than simply witnessing His acts.

The people saw this regular phenomenon and associated the cloud with divine glory. If so, then why did Moses continue agonizing for the full riches of His glory? (Exodus 33:18) The longing was not satisfied by the manifestation of a cloud over the Tent of Meeting. He still had a burden to experience something far greater.

Moses pleaded, "Lord, show me your *glory*!" and the Lord's reply clarifies the concept of holy splendor: "I will make all my *goodness* pass before you...." (Exodus 33:19) Glory is associated with goodness.

Jesus also connected goodness with glory when He said, "In the same way, let your light shine before others, so that they may see your *good* works and give *glory* to your Father who is in heaven." (Matthew 5:16) When followers of Jesus manifest goodness, they sense and others behold divine glory.

Later in the Sermon on the Mount, Jesus expresses an indirect association between God and goodness by saying, "If you, then, though you are evil, know how to give good gifts to your children, how much more will your *Father in heaven* give *good* gifts to those who ask him!" (Matthew 7:11) When asking for more of His presence,

His goodness is given.

The "riches of His glory" is the display of goodness, seen through compassion and mercy. His glory was seen when the late Mark Buntain, anointed by God and empowered by the Holy Spirit, touched the forsaken children of India with tireless love and devotion.

Many are looking for a *cloud* experience and missing His glory. Turn your heart to a child and to the Savior who said, "Suffer the little children to come unto Me!" and you see His glory.

Expressive praise in worship gatherings is wonderful, yet by feeding the hungry, clothing the naked, and visiting the prisoner, a follower of Jesus experiences the riches of His glory. By bringing the spiritually captive to an encounter with God and alleviating human suffering, people experience His glory.

Gain from the Father the riches of His glory. Display His goodness and acquire a profound sense of His fullness.

From the Holy Spirit: Strength (V.16)

Similar to conflict among people is unrest in the inner sanctum of the soul. The fullness of God includes inward strengthening by the Holy Spirit.

The Spirit of God wants to *strengthen* you. He has not come to make you *strong* but to be your *strength*. Becoming personally *strong* has never been part of the divine plan. If He came to only make you *strong* you could possibly conclude one day, "I have no further need of the Spirit, for now, I am strong." Constantly relying on His *strength* is what God desires.

Paul testified, "I can do all things through him who strengthens me." (Philippians 4:13) Believers must cling to the Lord at all times. They are to lean and depend on Him. Never is there a moment when a person should fail to rely upon the Holy Spirit. He desires to continually *strengthen* the children of God.

The strengthening of the Holy Spirit impacts three aspects of the heart:

Reasoning ability ends up deeply insightful, securing greater concentration for undertaking His purposes.

The *conscience*, the peace quotient of the heart, becomes extremely alert, reaping refined sensitivity for accomplishing His directives.

The *will* grows powerfully resolute, finding further determination for carrying out His plans.

Acquire from the Holy Spirit strength in the inner being. Rest in Him and resonant with divine fullness.

From the Son: Love (V.17)

Two dimensions of divine love are fully realized in the fullness of God.

First, the *vastness* of God's love. Paul wrote, "For I am sure that neither death nor life, nor angels nor rulers, nor things present nor things to come, nor powers, nor height nor depth, nor anything else in all creation, will be able to separate us from the love of God in Christ Jesus our Lord." (Romans 8:38-39)

The love of Christ is unconditional, comes without stipulations, has no addendums, and centers on *being* more than *doing*.

Paul features the unlimited capacity of love in Christ. (V. 18) The stated measurements were witnessed on the cross. Jesus demonstrated the complete scope of love by fully spreading out His arms to be crucified.

Jason Tuskes was a 17-year-old high school honor student. He had a very close relationship with his mother, his wheelchair-bound father, and his younger brother Christian. Jason was an expert swimmer who loved to scuba dive. He left home on a Tuesday morning to explore a spring and underwater cave near his home in west-central Florida. His plan was to be home in time to celebrate his mother's birthday.

Jason became lost in an underwater cave. In his panic, he got wedged into a narrow passageway. When he realized he was trapped, he shed his metal air tank, unsheathed his diver's knife and, with the tank as a tablet and the knife as a pen, wrote, "I love you, Mom, Dad, and Christian." He then ran out of air and drowned.

A dying message, something communicated in the

last seconds of life, cannot be ignored. God's final *Word* was etched in blood at Golgotha, screaming out the message, "My love is complete!"

Secondly, the *personal* nature of God's love. The vastness of divine love is extremely intimate and personal.

God has made known three circles of His love: Love for the world, the *universal* range of love; love for the church, the *community* scope of love; and love for the individual, the *personal* dimension of love.

No one loves a *multitude* like they do their *own child*. My wife and I sincerely love people but this does not compare to the love we have for our children and grandchildren. Love for family enters a personal level, impossible outside the home. Similarly, God loves the world but not like those adopted into His family.

To His own, He gives generously and unreservedly. His family gets the fullness. In the circle of personal love, He gives without restraint. Divine love is vast but the Heavenly Father wants you to experience His cherished affection through His Son.

Become full

Paul prayed for believers to enter the abundance of God and manifest His presence, experiencing complete restoration and total redemption. From the Father gain the riches of His glory. From the Holy Spirit become strengthened in the inner being. From the Son reap the benefits of personal love.

Seek to be filled with His fullness! Discover the ways of God rather than simply witnessing His acts. Regularly pray, "Lord, brings me beyond just *seeing* to fully knowing the *Source*."

CHAPTER EIGHT

MISSION

Now to him who is able to do far more abundantly than all that we ask or think, according to the power at work within us, to him be glory in the church and in Christ Jesus throughout all generations, forever and ever. Amen. (Ephesians 3:20-21)

The picture of the human condition in the world today is less than ideal. The social structure is being torn apart by hatred and strife. People are growing increasingly mean.

Nations are fighting nations, social and ethnic groups are opposing each other, individuals are bickering with one another. And within the human heart conflict is raging. The human condition can be brought into oneness in Christ. The church, the beloved community, is where a person can experience the limitless love of God, restoring peace.

The first half of the letter gives *foundation* to the structure of the covenant-community; the last half shows the way living by grace is *formulated*. Paul is about to transition out of *majestic* truths and enter *functional* realities.

The letter begins by showing the church is comprised of divinely called leaders and devoted followers of Jesus, blessed with spiritual blessings in heavenly places, growing in knowledge and holy wonder, relishing grace through faith in Christ, abiding together as a body and temple, showing genuine equality, and experiencing the fullness of God. He then concludes with a doxology; a statement of praise to the Lord capsulizing the church as the epicenter of worship.

The mission of the church is giving praise to God. By fulfilling the mission, the believer gains purpose. Mission and purpose are inner-connected.

The Church is more than a Way Station where someone receives rest and nourishment. Coming together is not just another item on a crowded appointment notepad. To treat connection with others as an option to an already busy schedule is not consistent with the design of the church. In Christ, God is the Author of time; not simply added but the actual agenda, fulfilling the concept of *Lordship*.

South Dakota has a couple of large Indian Reservations. Missionaries to the Lakota Nation have a great challenge. One of the bigger difficulties is helping people recognize Jesus as the *only* Lord. Many Native Americans find it extremely hard giving up multiple deities to serve the one True God.

Does this problem only apply to indigenous populations? Some people simply attempt to attach Jesus to their less than ideal lifestyle and fail to enter into an exclusive Lordship with Him. There is no peace of mind by simply making Him an attachment. Confessing "Jesus as Lord" (Romans 10:9) means he becomes your all in all.

Has Jesus simply become a *sedative* instead of the *Savior*? The soothing, calming, quieting effect many seek can only be gained by the calendar reflecting a change in priorities. Doing what was formerly done, living selfishly, and expecting to have the full wonder of peace connected to faith is impossible. Repentance means a change inside and out.

Conversion is not about developing a legalistic lifestyle but about living victoriously and abundantly. By professing Christ, a person becomes part of His church and the mission adds purpose to life. What is the intent behind engaging with others who follow Jesus?

Blessed to be a blessing

God desires to abundantly bless not only you but others *through* you. Everyone is to benefit from your life of faith. How?

Town and villages automatically benefit on account of the respectable behavior of believers. "When the *righteous* prosper, the *city* rejoices... Through the blessing of the *upright* a *city* is exalted...." (Proverbs 11:10, 11)

Nations also benefit on account of effective prayers. If *God's people* will be humble, pray, and seek His face, then He will hear, forgive, and heal *the land.* (2 Chronicles 7:14)

Why did God forgive your sins and bring you into a loving relationship with Him? Because He loves you? Yes! But also so you would invite others to come and know of His love.

Why has God blessed your occupation, your line of work? Because He cares for you? Yes! But also so you would have the means to spread the Good News. Believers "...must work, doing something useful with his own hands, that he *may have something to share...."* (Ephesians 4:28)

The LINKS Letter, a Christian publication to golfers, wrote: "We often believe that 10 percent of our money is His and the other 90 percent is ours. Everything we have belongs to Him, He owns it and we are simply stewards. Based on 2 Corinthians 9, some of what God gives us is *bread for food* and some is *seed for sowing.* The *bread for food* is for us to enjoy and be thankful. The purpose of the *seed for sowing* is to bless others in order to produce praise of thanksgiving to God through them. *That's the highest use of money.* And God promises He will increase the *seed for sowing.* Stewardship comes down to a matter of faith. Faith is not a single decision made years ago – it is *thousands* of choices made every day to believe that God will provide. When we exercise faith in our giving, we are basically saying, 'I choose one more time to believe that God is not lying.'"

Why does God fill believers with the Holy Spirit? Because He wants you to have more empowerment and greater strength to live victoriously? Yes! But also so you would have the increased ability to effectively tell His story to the uttermost parts of the earth.

Paul describes the incalculable blessing of God in three ways:

His blessing is *immeasurable* (V.20); superabundant, unrestrained, and extravagant by anyone's standards.

His blessing is *more than all we ask* (V.20); goes beyond what can be requested. Believers can spend eternity soliciting God on their knees, yet His blessing far exceeds any exhausting list of wishes.

His blessing is *more than all we imagine* (V.20); goes beyond human understanding, beyond what the mind can ponder and consider. Since no one can fully fathom the blessings of God, praying in the Spirit helps. Spirit praying opens the floodgates of unknowable blessings.

How can someone know God can deliver on this blessing? Because He *is able*. (V.20) Out of the *absoluteness* of His power, nothing is impossible.

The Lord confirms His ability by the working of the Spirit in your life. Recall what you were like before following Jesus and recognize the transformation that has already occurred. This same power is available for blessing others.

The covenant-community is blessed to fulfill the purpose of blessing others.

The extension of God's glory

The most accurate picture people can gain of God is from the church, His body. What portrait is being painted?

A missionary helped me better understand the challenges of telling others about Jesus in other parts of the world. The population where he serves is eighty-five percent Muslim and ten percent Hindu. Only ½ of 1 percent believe in Jesus. The people in his region know the United States was founded by Christians. They *assume* everything Americans do reflects Christianity.

Vulgar and obscene movies from Hollywood arrived in their country; they concluded Christianity is extremely immoral. American corporations came and employees were seen frequently drunk, visiting prostitutes, and treating others poorly; they concluded Christianity is of the devil.

The portrait of Jesus in many nations is the actions of the average American. Any wonder why telling others about Jesus globally can be so intensely problematic?

Now narrow the focus. You are His extended glory. You are a *walking Bible*. The only *Scripture* some will ever *read* is you. Are your next door neighbors and co-workers getting an accurate picture of God by you?

How are domestic tensions resolved in your home? Do they revert to shouting, sometimes leading to physical blows? How are problems at work handled? With lying and deception? How are issues in the church addressed? With gossip and malicious talk? The world often models unsavory behavior extremely well, yet those in Christ are to avoid such conduct.

The reputation of Jesus is in the hands of His followers. They are His reflection. Is your reflection of Him clean and clear?

When pastoring in Minnesota, my wife became good friends with a next door neighbor. Ann was a cheerful young mother and devoted wife. By American standards, Ann and Dave had a healthy and happy home.

After we moved to another part of the country, Brenda received an unexpected letter from Ann. She wrote about going to a church and coming to the altar to receive Christ. She thanked my wife for living like Jesus. Through Brenda, she came to realize something was missing in her life. The reflection of Jesus drew Ann to God.

Within the church, *Jesus* is the sphere of glory. Within the world, however, the *church* is the sphere of glory from which Jesus is seen. Who you are, what you say, and what you do, helps the world recognize Him. You are the extension of His glory to everyone until He returns.

Praise

On a wall near the main entrance of the Alamo in San Antonio, Texas is a portrait with the following inscription: "James Butler Bonham – no picture of him exists. This portrait is of his nephew, Major James Bonham, deceased, who greatly resembled his uncle. It is placed here by the family that people may know the appearance of the man who died for freedom."

No actual painting of Jesus exists. The likeness of the Son who died for eternal freedom is seen in the lives of those comprising the covenant-community. Show Jesus to others in every way possible.

The purpose of the church is twofold: Blessed to be a blessing and serving as an extension of His glory. When those comprising the covenant-community perform the mission of praising the Lord, they gain a deeply-seated desire to fulfill the purpose of blessing others and reflecting Jesus, discovering the true meaning of life.

CHAPTER NINE

WORTHY

I therefore, a prisoner for the Lord, urge you to walk in a manner worthy of the calling to which you have been called, with all humility and gentleness, with patience, bearing with one another in love, eager to maintain the unity of the Spirit in the bond of peace. (Ephesians 4:1-3)

Paul's letter about the covenant-community moves from the *theoretical* to the *operational*. For the church to be the beloved community the theory must work, the facts must function. Analysis must revert to action; *theology* must construct *truthfulness*, *doctrine* must generate *development*, and *revelation* must create *righteousness*.

The letter to the Ephesians starts by describing the Church. She is comprised of divinely called leaders and devoted followers of Jesus, blessed with spiritual blessings in heavenly places, on course but not yet complete, a grace society, a breathing organism and a sacred place, the only assembly of genuine equality, filled with the fullness of God, blessed to be a blessing, and the extension of His glory to the world. The church regularly gathers to experience the merciful Savior and the world comprehends Him by the mannerisms of His followers.

After Paul gives definition to the design of the covenant-community, he addresses the question: How is extravagant grace lived out? What are the practical elements weaved into the fiber of the breathing, pulsating, and sanctified church?

The first few lines of the second half of the letter provide the objective: "...to walk in a manner worthy of the calling." When people enter the covenant-community, they take upon themselves the *obligation* to live in a certain way. When someone fails, they hinder the advancement of the church and disgrace the name of Jesus.

Spiro Agnew, one-time Vice President of the United States, resigned from office in 1973 on charges of income tax evasion. He failed the *political community* by not living a life worthy of the civic calling and discredited the office of Vice President.

At Trinity Bible College student representatives were regularly sent to churches and regional youth events. Each member of the team had to commit themselves to upholding the standards of the school, regardless of personal preference. They had to agree to live a life worthy of the name of the institution. If they failed to accurately personify the *college community*, they tarnished the reputation of TBC.

When someone becomes a follower of Jesus, they become part of the Church. As a member of the *covenant-community*, they are to live in a worthy manner or they shame the fame of Jesus, her Lord.

Worthy means *bringing up the beams of the scales* and is associated with a weight balancing device. Lifestyle should weigh *as much as* or *be equal to* the declaration of faith. *Worthy* is about living with a balanced scale. *Walk* lines up with *talk*; *lifestyle* is in balance with *declaration*.

When the scale is balanced

Three qualities are seen when someone is living in a manner worthy of the calling.

First, *humility*! Humility comes out of an accurate knowledge of oneself.

One of the more humbling experiences of life happens when believers willingly and honestly examine themselves in the light of the perfect Lord. When comparing a lifestyle to divine perfection, shortcomings and imperfections are clearly revealed. Isaiah states self-righteousness, compared to God's holiness, appears filthy. (Isaiah 64:6)

The term *self-esteem* has become a popular expression and the new standard for viewing oneself. The term generates an element of discomfort by how it is enshrined, emphasizing self-ward focus and inward pride. The concept has some *harmful* connotations with just a couple *helpful* applications. What people need most is a good dose of *God-esteem*, recognizing their *deficiency* and gaining His *sufficiency*. The doorway to God-esteem is humility.

Some with faith in God take a position of *sinless perfection*, which can lead to pride. They perceive themselves completely free from all rebellious behavior.

A pastor was teaching a Bible study and mentioned that believers occasionally sin. A man began to arguably defend sinless perfection, convinced he was living sin-free on account of faith. He quarreled passionately and refused to stop. The minister, at wit's end, noticed a woman sitting next to him and inquired about her. The man indicated she was his wife. He then calmly and kindly asked, "Can I ask *her* if you're living a sinless life?" The debate ended and the man quietly sat down.

The scales of humility line up between *thinking too highly of yourself* and *tearing yourself down*. Balance the scales! See life in comparison to Jesus instead of by the opinion of others. Gain esteem by depending on Him for overcoming power.

Secondly, *gentleness*! Gentleness is the opposite of self-assertion.

Aristotle, the classic thinker and teacher, compared gentleness as the balance between being *too angry* and *never angry*. He defined gentleness as *always angry at the right time and never angry at the wrong time*. Anger has a purposeful role in the design of righteous attributes. The right time for anger is seeing others suffer and the wrong time is when personally suffering.

Scripture indicates Moses was the meekest (*gentlest*) man to ever live. (Numbers 12:3) He possessed a balance in the handling of anger; angry when people acted shamefully toward God and never angry when people acted shamefully toward him. Yet, His testimony also includes a time when he failed to balance the scales, angrily striking instead of speaking to a rock. The result was an inability to enter the promises of God. (Numbers 20:11-12)

When someone stabilizes gentleness, every passion is under perfect control. The person is always angry at the right time and never angry at the wrong time.

Thirdly, *forbearance*! Paul wrote, "...patience, bearing with one another in love." The phrase communicates patience but much more. The comparable word *forbearance* conveys the depth of patience required for balancing the scales.

Forbearance is having *the power to retaliate but never exercising it*. Forbearance is having a position of strength and not initiating an attack. Forbearance involves the refusal to take revenge. Forbearance bears insult and injury without bitterness and complaint. One description of forbearance is *suffering unpleasant people with graciousness and fools without irritation.*

Some believers never pray for patience, thinking situations only grow worse. Others pray and expect or demand immediate results. Patience, however, is developed through prolonged periods of time, involving constant dialogue with the Lord. The weights of annoyance, frustration, aggravation, and exasperation, working against the weights of humbleness and gentleness, adds substance to forbearance and the right balance of grace living.

These three qualities, when seen in a believer, reveals a life worthy of the calling; *behavior* is aligned with *confession*.

When the scale is out of balance

Efforts must be made by everyone to preserve unity or the quality of grace living declines, the scales start to tilt. Believers are to be *eager* to maintain "the unity of the Spirit in the bond of peace." (V.3)

When unity is out of balance, clamoring and dissension soon follow. But when everyone balances the scale with humility, gentleness, and forbearance, the oneness fashioned by the Lord is *upheld*. Followers of Jesus do not *create* unity; it is established by individually manifesting His attributes and collectively abiding in Christ.

In a story written about arctic wolves, a seven-member pack targeted several oxen calves, guarded by eleven grown oxen. As the wolves approached their quarry the oxen bunched in an impenetrable semicircle, their deadly hooves facing out. The calves remained safe during the long standoff.

A single ox broke rank and the herd scattered into nervous little groups. A skirmish ensued. The grown oxen finally fled in panic and the calves were left to the mercy of the predators. Not a single calf survived.

The enemy of your soul continues to attack the church, yet she cannot be penetrated and destroyed when unity is maintained. When followers of Jesus break ranks, when believers personally fail to balance the scales with humility, gentleness, and forbearance, the covenant-community becomes easy prey.

Oneness

Unity does not mean *uniformity*. Having oneness in Christ does not take away personal identity. Paul described the church as similar to the human body, having uniquely different members. (1 Corinthians 12) The covenant-community is very diverse.

Harold Carter, one-time pastor of New Shiloh Baptist Church in Baltimore, Maryland analyzed the beloved community by saying, "The church is the Bride of Christ. We do not like seeing our own bride always wearing the same dress. God likes seeing His Bride in an assortment of clothing as well."

Forty-three different church affiliations in America

brand themselves *Pentecostal* in belief. Some point to *speaking in tongues* as the sole evidence of the baptism in the Holy Spirit, others are open to various kinds of signs. Equally, some groups are determined to see the church go through the Great Tribulation while others recognize the wrath of God is against sin, the church being forgiven and delivered. God will clear-up every difference of opinion when those following Jesus are in His presence. Until then, Pentecostal believers are to urgently strive to preserve oneness, given by the same Holy Spirit to everyone.

In a classic *Peanuts* cartoon, Lucy was standing with her arms folded, having a resolute look on her face. Charlie Brown was pleading, "Lucy, you MUST be more loving. This world needs love. You have to let yourself love to make the world a better place in which to live!" Lucy whirls around angrily, causing Charlie Brown to do a backward flip, and screams, "Look, blockhead – the world I love, it's the people I can't stand" Are believers following *her* lead instead of *Jesus*, loving the church but not one another?

The first part of the letter ended by emphasizing *blessed to be a blessing*. Nothing destroys blessing more quickly than dissension. When this happens, not much is left for blessing others.

Worthy

A sea captain and chief engineer were arguing over who was most important to the ship. To prove their individual worth, they decided to swap places for a voyage. The chief engineer ascended to the bridge and the captain went to the engine room.

Several hours later the captain suddenly appeared on the deck covered with oil and dirt. "Chief!" he yelled waving a monkey wrench, "You have got to get down there. I can't make her go!"

"Of course you can't," replied the chief, "She's run aground!"

The church is sometimes described as a gospel ship. Children's ministries in various churches even use seafaring titles, such as "Heaven's Harbor Children's Church" and "Wee Care Wharf." When everyone lives in humility, gentleness, and forbearance (worthy of the calling), unity is preserved and the *gospel ship* does not end up motionless and useless.

Are you living a worthy life and honoring His name? Are you in the right disposition to preserve unity? If not, it is time to balance the scales.

CHAPTER TEN

COMMON

There is one body and one Spirit—just as you were called to the one hope that belongs to your call—one Lord, one faith, one baptism, one God and Father of all, who is over all and through all and in all. But grace was given to each one of us according to the measure of Christ's gift. Therefore it says, "When he ascended on high he led a host of captives, and he gave gifts to men." (In saying, "He ascended," what does it mean but that he had also descended into the lower regions, the earth? He who descended is the one who also ascended far above all the heavens, that he might fill all things.) And he gave the apostles, the prophets, the evangelists, the shepherds and teachers, to equip the saints for the work of ministry, for building up the body of Christ, until we all attain to the unity of the faith and of the knowledge of the Son of God, to mature manhood, to the measure of the stature of the fullness of Christ, so that we may no longer be children, tossed to and fro by the waves and carried about by every wind of doctrine, by human cunning, by craftiness in deceitful schemes. Rather, speaking the truth in love, we are to grow up in every way into him who is the head, into Christ, from whom the whole body, joined and held together by every joint with which it is equipped, when each part is working properly, makes the body grow so that it builds itself up in love. (Ephesians 4:4-16)

The first section of the letter *describes* the design of the church. The last section *reveals* grace living within the beloved community. Humility, gentleness, and forbearance are to *balance the scales* of grace in every believer. By these three qualities working in sync with each other, they help bring oneness to the covenant-community, a unity of the Spirit established by the Father and preserved in Christ.

Uniqueness receives a lot of attention today. Self-made and one-of-a-kind people are highly praised. In an effort to rise above others, special attention is often given to remarkable abilities and talents. Someone is considered outstanding by what they alone possess. Does this cause needless resentment within the covenant-community?

The government of England contains two legislative branches, the House of *Lords* and the House of *Commons*. The House of Lords is comprised of ancient landowners and nobility. Presently, they have very little of their original authority. Like the royal family, their service is limited. The actual rule of the land is the House of Commons.

Commonality is a word meaning to *possess, along with others, a certain set of attributes*. Instead of underlining extraordinary qualities, the unity of the Spirit promotes what is held in common. *Community* and *commonality* are singular in purpose, heightening *oneness*. The covenant-community shows divine authority as the church of commoners, a convergence of oneness birth by common characteristics.

Pointing out differences easily happens among churches. A local congregation sometimes promotes herself above other churches by highlighting distinctions. Groups define and sub-define themselves with various terms; such as Orthodox, Catholic, Protestant, Mainstream, Liberal, Conservative, Evangelical, and Pentecostal. Some alliances declare themselves a Movement rather than a Denomination, suggesting a more superior, faster growing, or further advancing association. Unfortunately, arrogance swiftly chases and often closes the gap behind such elusive designations.

Many have heard the well-worn folklore about Saint Peter giving a group of new arrivals a tour of heaven. Coming upon a wall someone asked, "Why the wall?" Peter replied, "The Baptists are on the other side and think they are the only ones here." This, however, is not just a problem with only one group. Most groups struggle with feelings of supremacy. A Gideon Bible representative said to me once, "I'm a Lutheran first and a Christian second."

God is not opposed to diverse groupings. More has

been accomplished for the cause of Christ through these forms of structure than by any other means. But with sundry titles come unnecessary walls.

If a person indicates they are a Christian, a follow-up question is usually asked: "What kind? What is your church affiliation?"

In earlier trips to the Holy Land my wife and I hosted group tours. Isaac, an Orthodox Jew from Tel Aviv, always served as our local guide. While riding on the bus to a Biblical site, he made a reference to Christians in our private conversation, placing everyone in the same category. I tried to explain the distinctions among Christians. He looked at me and said, "You all believe in Jesus, don't you? Then you're all Christians!" End of discussion! In other words, Christ is the commonality of every covenant-community.

Commonality births community

The majesty of oneness is found in grace living.

One Body! The Body of Christ is the interconnection among followers of Jesus, showing their dependence upon one another.

One Spirit! The Greek word for Spirit, *pneuma*, is the root of the English word *pulmonary*, referring to lungs and breathing. The *pneuma* of the Holy Spirit, the *breath* of God, brings life to the Body of Christ.

Similar to the Lord miraculously breathing the

breath of life into the first human at creation (Genesis 2:7), the blowing wind on the day of Pentecost (Acts 2:2) was the *breath of grace living* powerfully entering the newly born Body of Christ.

Breathing, however, is not a one-time experience. Once breathing stops, the body dies. The Holy Spirit has come to continually breathe life into the covenant-community.

One hope! Grace living is done with a sense of expectation and confidence.

One Lord! The beloved church is fully yielded to the Lordship of Jesus and completely devoted to living by grace.

One faith! Trusting Christ brings complete and dynamic access to grace living.

One baptism! Fully immersed in Christ, the streams of forgiveness and compassion overflow the banks of grace living.

One God! Commonality is fully experienced in the one True God. By holding everything in common, a clear and accurate testimony of grace living is witnessed. (Acts 4:32-35)

Wonderful blessings are experienced when followers of Jesus have one mind, one heart, and one passion. By living in one accord a personal implosion and corporate explosion of joy occur and liberty in the Spirit becomes fully engaged.

Commonality develops community

Divine gifts are referred to in three of Paul's writings. The letter to the Romans mentions natural *motivational* gifts, increasing the capacity for effectiveness in communication, leadership, organization, generosity, nurture, and instruction. (Romans 12:4-8)

The letter to the Corinthians highlights supernatural *ministry* gifts, manifesting uncanny insight, intervention, and inspiration, activated according to the need of the moment. (1 Corinthians 12:8-11)

The letter to the Ephesians addresses unifying *mentoring* gifts, shaping the oneness of grace living. (Vs. 11-12) These gifts have been mistakenly considered *five* dimensional yet the grammatical structure of the original language only expresses *four*.

Out of the realm of commonality and oneness, these gifts *serve a function* in the covenant-community instead of *designate an office*. A person functions as an apostle or prophet or evangelist or pastor-teacher, rather than hold a position of governance using these designated titles.

The apostolic ministry! Paul references *Apostles*. Scripture makes a distinction between *The Twelve* and other recognized *apostles*, one being Paul. Although there is a lot of speculation about their function, one pattern is clearly evident; they pursue unreached people groups with intense passion and start additional Churches of the

Beloved.

Various church networks refer to themselves as apostolic, seeking to engage every nation with the message of Jesus. Presently some, not all, global missionaries are performing an apostolic ministry.

The prophetic ministry! Paul also references *Prophets*. These individuals provide counsel and encouragement more than render guidance and direction. Occasionally they foretell divine plans and objectives, yet more often their comments expose sin and bring clarity to current events.

The evangelistic ministry! Paul references *Evangelists*. Every follower of Jesus has the assignment to tell others His story, yet some are better able to more effectively connect with the unconverted. They candidly present the Good News and redirect the rebellious in right directions. These individuals are more inclined toward *quantity*, wanting the masses to come to Christ.

The training ministry! Paul references *Pastor-teachers*, the shepherd-instructors serving within the covenant-community. Believers need to be given regular and ongoing attention, involving guidance, nourishment, correction, cleansing, and protection. Those in the training ministry have a shepherd's heart, possessing the scent of humanity but giving off an odor of holiness. They are naturally inclined toward *quality*, preparing a pure and praiseworthy covenant-community.

The four ministries are not listed in order of

importance but of necessity. The *Apostle* searches out the harvest fields of lost humanity, the *Prophet* exposes defiance and rebellion, the *Evangelist* highlights the remedy, and the *Pastor-teacher* equips the devoted followers. In other words, Apostles break up hard soil, Prophets plant good seed, Evangelists reap a bountiful harvest, and Pastor-teachers clean and process the fruit, making it beneficial for the Kingdom of God. These enduring ministries broaden the length, height, breadth, and depth of grace living. (3:18)

Commonality advances community

The people of God are admonished to keep the unity of the Spirit (V.3) until a unity of the faith is achieved (V.13). The church is progressing *from* one level of unity *to* a more advanced form of unity.

The fourfold ministry guides the church in a twofold way to a comprehensive unity.

The fourfold ministry prepares believers for works of service. (V.12) The word *prepare* carries the idea of putting something into the right position, as it ought to be, building up instead of tearing down. Grace living is strengthened by every follower of Jesus actively serving the Lord. The goal is for everyone to broaden the scope of His message.

The fourfold ministry also helps believers mature. (V.13) Maturity produces *stability*, individuals no longer tossed back and forth or blown here and there. Maturity also fights against the *craftiness* of wicked people in their deceitful schemes. (V.14)

Paul used the word *cunning*, a word referencing dice throwing. The Greek term is "kubeia," where the English word *cube* originates. A clever cheat can hold two sets of dice in their hand and throw whichever set they desire. Tricksters use *crafty* methods (sleight of hands; a quick switch) in an effort to fool the *unstable*. Maturity, however, deters falling into deceit.

Those following Jesus are to pursue the profound oneness contained in the orbit of *Spirit* and *faith*. With greater depths of maturity, the covenant-community becomes joined and held together by each supporting function. Unified advancement comes out of the integrated and synchronized experience of abundant grace living. (V.16)

Oneness has an aim

A television talk show had a body builder as a guest. The host asked, "Why do you develop your muscles? The person simply stepped forward and flexed a series of well-defined muscles from chest to calf. The audience applauded.

The host asked, "What do you use all those muscles for?"

Again, the muscular specimen flexed. Biceps and triceps sprouted to impressive proportions.

The host persisted, "But what do you use those

muscles for?"

The body builder did not have a clue of what the host was asking. All he knew to do was display a well-developed frame.

Improvement is not simply for posing to an audience. Admiring and applauding spectacular achievements are not associated with the unifying power of grace living.

The fourfold ministry of the covenant-community has a function. Development must end with service. Maturity must bring steadiness. Those following Jesus are to fulfill meaningful ministry by engaging their world of influence with His story!

CHAPTER ELEVEN

STANDARDS

Now this I say and testify in the Lord, that you must no longer walk as the Gentiles do, in the futility of their minds. They are darkened in their understanding, alienated from the life of God because of the ignorance that is in them, due to their hardness of heart. They have become callous and have given themselves up to sensuality, greedy to practice every kind of impurity. But that is not the way you learned Christ!—assuming that you have heard about him and were taught in him, as the truth is in Jesus, to put off your old self, which belongs to your former manner of life and is corrupt through deceitful desires, and to be renewed in the spirit of your minds, and to put on the new self, created after the likeness of God in true righteousness and holiness. (Ephesians 4:17-24)

Paul begins the second half of the letter by blending *individualism* with *oneness*. His next topic is uniform *standards.*

The goodness of mankind is the preferred focus of the general public. When the days of creation were complete, the Lord said, "It was very good!" (Genesis 1:31). the optimum word in His pronouncement being "was."

Since the great rebellion in the Garden of Eden. Scripture highlights a different assessment: "For all have sinned and come short of the glory of God." (Romans 3:23) Regardless the original design. disobedience planted the *seed* of sin that eventually sprouted into *acts* of sin.

When someone places faith in God. the sinful nature is not removed but covered. and they experience the blessing of *atonement*. The sacrificial blood of Jesus shed on Mount Calvary *atones* for sin and *covers* transgressions. By the indwelling of the Holy Spirit. while the sinful nature is still present. the power of sin is broken. Believers are no longer *governed* by sin. though they may still occasionally *grapple* with transgressions.

In the classic story. *In His Steps*. a local congregation decides to do nothing without first answering the question, "What would Jesus do?" Believers should earnestly endeavor to behave more like Jesus in attitude and actions. yet no one will live a *perfect* life in a wrecked world, only a *forgiven* life.

False assumptions often form a dark cloud over grace, causing shadows of deceit. Some assume grace living allows them to behave as they did before placing faith in God. Without the tangible benefit of heart-change, grace lacks essence. The unchanged life still contends with guilt, shame, and lack of peace. Those following Jesus are to enter transformation, the renewal of the mind, and live free of internal turmoil and chaos. Faith means having an intimate relationship with God by severing ties with sin.

Paul helps the beloved community to recognize the standards of grace, very different from the norms of the surrounding culture. Followers of Jesus are to no longer live "as the Gentiles do," in futile thinking. (V.17)

A clear contrast does exist between *sinner* and *saint* and, depending on the mindset of the individual, a chain reaction is triggered in one or the other arena. The sin-ward slide will occur instinctively while the saint-ward climb is done intentionally.

Steps to becoming a worse sinner

All sinners sin but some are viler. No man or woman becomes an extreme sinner instantly.

The process starts with *futile* thinking, empty thoughts lacking substance when examined in the light of eternity. (V.17)

The process develops to a *darkened* understanding. (V.18) Ignorance increases and the individual moves blindly in a delusional world.

The process moves deeper into a *hardened* heart. (V.18) The Greek word "paresis" is from the word *paras*, a material harder than marble. A carnal chalkstone forms in the joints of the soul, tougher than the skeletal support structure itself, *paralyzing* actions and eventually crippling attitudes.

The process ends with a *loss* of all sensitivity. (V.19) Life becomes *calloused*. It develops a thick veneer unable to sense danger. Just as thick tissue prevents the skin from foreseeing potential injury, radical defiance blocks the soul from anticipating deadly consequences.

Young people often seek to be considered *cool, hip, or with it*, according to the standards of their peers. In the late 50's and early 60's, if someone achieved recognition they were *groovy*, traveling in the popular ruts of the latest trends. In an era when destructive experiences, detrimental activities, and denigrating language were growing in admiration, teenagers refusing such behavior were out of tune, or not in sync, with eroding norms. Actually, their heart was not yet hardened by demoralizing standards.

While working as a Glazer (glass cutter), my co-workers had very foul-mouths. I could not escape the environment of constant obscenities and grew increasingly alarmed about the possibility of becoming callous toward crude language. Would an inappropriate word unintentionally slip out of my mouth in front of my children? Driving home from work became a 15-minute conversation with God, asking for a purging of my mind of all profanity.

An area growing increasingly insensitive in society involves cruelty. Indifference towards violence is intensifying, whether in computer games, featured movies, or various sports.

The classic movie *Jurassic Park* is mild in comparison to many levels of brutality often commonplace today. When first released the show became a box office sensation. The film was a major topic on television talk shows. Children flocked to the theater. Parents were amazed by the technological imagery.

My wife and I became curious but hesitated to view the film. A trusted friend gave us his opinion, making us feel more comfortable about watching the movie. We rented the video. My wife and I were shocked by the terror. The attack of dinosaurs and the mutilated body parts was gruesome. We concluded the average American family has grown increasingly numb toward savagery.

Sin has petrifying effects. Transgressions once regarded with horror and considered repulsive, move to simply being resisted. Eventually, a sense of wrongness evaporates and they start becoming justified. Finally, rebellion, once rejected, is done freely and frequently, satisfying every kind of impurity. (V.19)

Three terrible outcomes come from living *as the Gentiles do*: sin becomes dominant, shame becomes lost, and decency becomes forgotten. The heart hardens and loses a sense of wrongfulness. Wayward desires destroy innocence and cause eternal damage.

Steps to becoming a better saint

Sinners innately worsen and, sadly, some saints fail to improve. Some tangible *action steps* are required in order to develop a greater sense of Jesus. Those having faith in God should be able to look at their past and say, "I *used to* live in accordance with degrading values but not anymore."

Discovering Christ is complete at *conversion*. A person becomes forgiven, Jesus becomes Lord, and a believer becomes a saint. Yet moving from initial *grace* to *grace living* is not finished, the process continues. Three adventures produce greater transformation.

First, *putting off the old self.* (V.22) Followers of Jesus deny themselves the base cravings resident in rebellion and arrogance.

The areas of resistance are different for each individual. For example, some people crave chocolate: not a problem for me. Denying chocolate is personally easy. Yet offer a piece of white cake with white frosting and I become vulnerable.

Similarly, many struggle with greed, some with inappropriate pleasures, and others with fame. Flaws sometimes overlap or interconnect. Efforts must be made to cast aside every immoral and amoral outlook. What weaknesses of your previous disposition must you *put off?*

Secondly, *gaining a new outlook.* (V.23) People who live for temporal indulgences and fleeting happiness often end up disappointed, leading to grumbling and even bitterness. The Holy Spirit has come to create new models of thinking in believers, to help them reason differently, moving them from *grumbling* to *gratefulness.* The new divine makeover involves giving thanks in all circumstances. (1 Thessalonians 5:18) Living for God impacts thought patterns.

At a training conference, the list of speakers was a *who's who* in Christian ministries. A speaker for one of the workshops wished to emphasize a point and illustrated a good principle with inappropriate language. The audience was shocked. Why were they flabbergasted? Because the audience no longer thought in that manner. The speaker, however, was unable to say, "I used to think crudely but not anymore."

Finally, *putting on the new self,* which involves righteousness and holiness. (V.24) Consider once again the premise behind asking the question, what would Jesus do? Before viewing demoralizing pictures and videos, what would Jesus do? Before attending faith-destroying events, what would Jesus do? Before consuming harmful chemicals or indulging in inebriating beverages, what would Jesus do? Before stealing at the workplace or taking merchandise from a store, what would Jesus do? Before driving recklessly and endangering others, what would Jesus do? Before abusing and exploiting people, what would Jesus do?

When my two sons were young, I planned a wilderness adventure for the three of us. Iron Creek Lake in the Black Hills of South Dakota is a wonderful spot for camping and enjoying the great outdoors. The lake is nestled in the northern hills close to an abandoned mining town. The waters are filled with Rainbow Trout.

Loaded with camping gear, fishing poles, and light artillery, we headed up the gravel logging road. The site has very few amenities. Bathing and getting cleaned-up is very difficult and inconvenient. We *men* decided this event would forego shaving and showering. The three of us came home filthy. My wife took one look at us and pointed to the bathroom. After a thorough washing, the visible results were amazing.

The radical transformation realized in Christ involves coming to Him in dirty and smelly carnality, being guided to the cleansing waves of grace, and putting on the freshly scented clothes of righteousness. God wants to give your soul a radical renovation. He not only desires to be the Author of your life but the Pattern of your living.

Sinner or saint

Many campers choose to vacation in motor homes. They put all the conveniences of their house on wheels. There is no contending with tents, sleeping bags, campfires, and outhouses. They just park their *home* in the midst of trees and hook up the water line, sewer hose, and electrical unit. Unable to live without television, some even mount a satellite dish.

People buy a motor home to see new places yet deck it out with favorite furnishings. In other words, nothing really changes. They drive to a new place and set themselves in new surroundings, but the newness is unnoticed on account of the cozy stuff carried with them.

Grace living comes with honor producing standards. The adventures of a new life in Jesus begins when the comfortable patterns of the old nature are left behind.

The process of becoming a worse sinner transitions from a hardened heart, to a loss of shame, to a preference for damaging pleasures. The process of becoming a better saint is connected to casting off sin, thinking differently, and putting on the righteousness of Christ.

CHAPTER TWELVE

TENSION

Therefore, having put away falsehood, let each one of you speak the truth with his neighbor, for we are members one of another. Be angry and do not sin; do not let the sun go down on your anger, and give no opportunity to the devil. Let the thief no longer steal, but rather let him labor, doing honest work with his own hands, so that he may have something to share with anyone in need. Let no corrupting talk come out of your mouths, but only such as is good for building up, as fits the occasion, that it may give grace to those who hear. And do not grieve the Holy Spirit of God, by whom you were sealed for the day of redemption. Let all bitterness and wrath and anger and clamor and slander be put away from you, along with all malice. Be kind to one another, tenderhearted, forgiving one another, as God in Christ forgave you. (Ephesians 4:25-32)

In grace living, three things are noted by Paul: The

individual lifestyle is humility, gentleness, and forbearance. *community unity* is found by emphasizing common characteristics, and *uniform standards* begin by no longer living as the Gentles do. Believers are to put off the old self, have a new outlook, and put on a new self, engulfed by righteousness and holiness. He now adds a few more comments about *standards*.

On one of my trips to the Holy Land, I had a conversation in Jerusalem with a Messianic Jew, an extremely small segment of the Jewish population. We talked about the living conditions for Israelis who believe in Christ. I learned they do not refer to themselves as Messianic Jews because the Orthodox Jew is deeply offended. They say they are *Jews who believe in Jesus*.

I, too, minimize using a term: the label *Christian*. The expression has come to represent institutionalized faith, a formalized commitment. Abiding in Christ should be fresh and renewing. A more accurate phrase that expresses love for God is *Christ follower* or *follower of Jesus*. Instead of a religious institution designing and establishing the norm for every situation, the question should be, "What would Jesus do?" Christ is the standard-bearer instead of seemingly pious legislative decrees.

Tension is the interplay between conflicting elements, often causing mental, emotional, and physical strain. Putting on the *new self* creates new tensions. Faith in God does not eliminate tension as much as creates different types of unease. Life in a broken world will always have rudiments of trauma yet faith in God becomes deeper by these experiences.

The world is damaged and people whose lives have been genuinely repaired in Christ are quickly recognized in such fractured surroundings. Developing into an even greater likeness of Jesus involves new pressures and the Holy Spirit helps a person handle the discomfort.

Paul cautions believers about the possibility of offending the Spirit of God. (V.30) In Luke 12 the Holy Spirit is *blasphemed*. In Acts 5 the Holy Spirit is *lied to*. In Acts 7 the Holy Spirit is *resisted*. In 1 Thessalonians 5 the Holy Spirit can be *quenched*. In Hebrews 10 the Holy Spirit can be treated with *contempt*. And, in Ephesians 4 the Holy Spirit can be *grieved*. Grieving the Spirit occurs when someone wrongly yields to everyday tensions.

Truthfulness or falsehood

"Having put away falsehood, let each one of you speak the truth." (V.25)

After high school, I wanted to sell my car before joining the Air Force, a 1954 Ford sedan. The vehicle had a 3-speed column stick-shift and 6-cylinder engine with manual overdrive. A large amount of oil would dump on the ground every time the motor was turned off. The car started only by compression (no problem for the hills of Seattle). The radiator leaked terribly. White smoke filled the air while going down the road. The movie "Uncle Buck" shows the perfect example of my first automobile while driving. Despite all the deficiencies, the vehicle was fairly reliable transportation.

A man saw my ad in the newspaper and came to take a look. We went for a drive. The car quickly started by compression and I hoped he would not notice out of the rear view mirror the amount of smoke billowing from the exhaust pipe.

He decided to buy the automobile. We went into the house to finish the transaction. My dad came into the kitchen and started talking to him about my old Ford.

"Now the car has a leaky radiator."

"The rear main seal is bad and the engine loses a lot of oil."

"The starter doesn't work."

He listed every problem. I could not believe he was torpedoing the sale. Yet the guy still bought the vehicle.

After the buyer left, my dad said, "Never give an opportunity for someone to think less of you." Truth involves both what is *said* and what is purposely *omitted*.

Falsehood grieves the Holy Spirit. Falsehood is failing to actually be what people think you are, a phony. Falsehood is saying things leading people to erroneous perceptions. Falsehood is gaining respect by deception.

Cell phones are presently a way of life but at one time they were a rare novelty. When first introduced to the general public, the item was extremely expensive. Only people with financial means could easily afford one.

A manufacturer decided to create *fake* cell phones. Although they looked authentic they did not work. The company advertised the product by saying, "It is not what you own but what people think you own that matters." Can you imagine someone asking to use your cell phone and having to tell them it is a toy?

Falsehood involves spending so much time lying about yourself that you end up not knowing the truth and start believing a lie. A saying is often used when commenting about someone puffed up with a false perception of themselves: "They are believing their own Press Release!" (a normally amplified perspective). Make sure this cannot be said of you.

Truth upholds grace living while falsehood destroys.

Anger or wrath

"Be *angry* and do not sin; do not let the sun go down on your *anger*." (V.26) The English Standard Version of the Bible uses the word "anger" twice, yet in the original language two different words are recorded. The first expresses *anger* while the second conveys *wrath*.

Anger was expressed when Jesus turned over the tables at the temple. (Mark 11:15) Injustice generated anger. Likewise, evil scheming should be irritating to those following Jesus. Sinful practices should cause outrage.

The other word, *wrath*, is a graver form of anger, seething with *bitterness* or *resentment*. The worst part of wrath is the way it quickly turns into a foothold of the devil, an opportunity he gladly capitalizes on.

Scripture records two enraged moments in the life of Moses. The first happened while holding two tablets of timeless directives. (Exodus 32:19) His soul was stirred by zeal for the Lord. He was *angry* over the immoral acts of the people and quickly acted to restore honorable behavior.

The second occurred while people were grumbling in the wilderness. (Numbers 20:2-13) They had become an irritation to Moses. The chronic complaining worked resentment in his heart. He disobeyed God, struck out with *wrath*, and dishonored the Lord.

Anger restores grace living while wrath discredits.

Steal or labor

"Let the thief no longer steal, but rather let him labor, doing honest work with his own hands." (V.28) Believers are to do everything within their means to provide for the needs of themselves and their household. They should also attempt to budget funds for helping others.

God does not raise lazy children. Those following Jesus should be some of the best workers in the workplace, employees with the highest levels of integrity.

Stealing takes many forms. Shoplifting and burglary are obviously wrong but have you considered the following: Loafing on the job while others work; undue or prolonged breaks; coming late or leaving early; using company supplies for personal use; expecting others to do your duties; receiving benefits not entitled?

A newly credentialed minister was hoping to preach at the denomination's national conference. He kept pestering the chairman for an opportunity. Out of frustration, the chairman decided to teach the young man a lesson. He was given the privilege of addressing the convention the night before the chairman was scheduled to speak. He was hoping the inexperienced minister would fail miserably and humiliate himself.

The young preacher thought and thought but could not come up with an appropriate topic. Growing increasingly alarmed over the situation, he went to the chairman the day before his speaking engagement and asked for advice. The chairman with an element of satisfaction counseled him, "The Lord will provide!"

The guy went to the convention hall to earnestly pray. He noticed the chairman's sermon notes sitting on the pulpit and thought this was an answer to prayer. The next night he preached the chairman's sermon flawlessly and the people gave him a standing ovation.

The chairman came to him absolutely furious, "You stole my sermon. You made the audience think it was yours. Now, what am I supposed to do." The young man replied, "The Lord will provide; the Lord will provide!"

Stealing time, opportunity, effort, and provisions disgraces grace living.

Edify or corrupt

"Let no corrupting talk come out of your mouths, but only such as is good for building up, as fits the occasion, that it may give grace to those who hear." (V.29)

Paul highlights communication for the second time. The first addresses *accuracy*, truth or falsehood; the second addresses *intent*, edify or destroy.

Words that edify and encourage others honor the Lord. An age-old adage is worth repeating, "If you can't say anything good, don't say anything at all." If seasoned with grace, constructive criticism can be productive. Followers of Jesus should carefully avoid speaking for the sake of demeaning others.

Corrupt talk literally means *putrid, rotten, unwholesome, filthy, and rancid*. In other words, avoid laxity in vocabulary. Has vulgarity and crudeness slipped into your normal way of speaking? When angry or hurt what comes out of your mouth? What is said when you accidently stub your toe, knock your shin, or injure your thumb?

Nasty communication damages grace living.

Bitter or kind

"Let all bitterness...be put away from you." (V.31) "Be kind to one another, tenderhearted...." (V.32) Attitudes count as much as actions. Everyone chooses both their mindset and behavior.

Jesus was asked, "How many times do I have to forgive someone? Seven times?" He responded, "Seventy times seven!" (Matthew 18:21-22) Does this mean revenge becomes possible at offense number 491? No! Jesus is saying, "Regardless the frequency, forgiveness must always reign."

Several expressions relate to bitterness. Bitterness expresses *resentment*. Rage is bitterness expressed as a *violent outburst*. Wrath is bitterness expressed as *impulsive behavior*. Brawling is bitterness expressed as *shouting*. Slander is bitterness expressed as *blasphemy*. Malice is bitterness expressed as *ill-feeling*.

Bitterness in every expression degrades grace living.

Tensions

Tensions are on-going and lifelong: truthfulness or falsehood, anger or wrath, work or steal, build or destroy, forgiveness or bitterness. These actions can either develop or dishonor grace living.

To master every disquieting situation that requires a choice to be made, seek help from the Holy Spirit. He wants to come alongside and render aid. If you *fail* to call for assistance, He *grieves* over your decision.

CHAPTER THIRTEEN

CONTRAST

Therefore be imitators of God, as beloved children. And walk in love, as Christ loved us and gave himself up for us, a fragrant offering and sacrifice to God. But sexual immorality and all impurity or covetousness must not even be named among you, as is proper among saints. Let there be no filthiness nor foolish talk nor crude joking, which are out of place, but instead let there be thanksgiving. For you may be sure of this, that everyone who is sexually immoral or impure, or who is covetous (that is, an idolater), has no inheritance in the kingdom of Christ and God. Let no one deceive you with empty words, for because of these things the wrath of God comes upon the sons of disobedience. Therefore do not become partners with them; for at one time you were darkness, but now you are light in the Lord. Walk as children of light (for the fruit of light is found in all that is good and right and true), and try to discern what is pleasing to the Lord. Take no part in the unfruitful works of darkness, but instead expose them. For it is shameful even to speak of the things that they do in secret. But when anything is exposed by the light, it becomes visible, for anything that becomes visible is light. Therefore it says, "Awake, O sleeper, and arise from the dead, and Christ will shine on you." (Ephesians 5:1-14)

The key phrase for the last half of the letter is "walk in a manner worthy of the calling," (4:1) involving individual *lifestyle,* community *unity,* and uniform *standards.*

When following Jesus, tensions occur in a broken world. Day-by-day and moment-by-moment, those loving God must determine what conflicting element is going to influence behavior.

Paul now transitions from the subject of *tensions* to *contrast,* the contrast between past and present, the difference between darkness and light. Grace living causes definite changes, needing constant and further development. Is there clear evidence of no longer living as before?

Tension is created by no longer living as the Gentiles do while *contrast* is seen by imitating God and living a life of love. (Vs. 1-2) The Greek word translated *imitators* is where the English word *mimic* originates, a term literally meaning *follower.* Just as growing from an infant into adulthood is a long gradual process of duplicating the actions of parents, *following* Jesus involves similar progressions.

How is this accomplished? By regulating behavior in the sphere of love! As God is love, then imitate, mimic, follow, and manifest Him. The catalyst of change is divine love.

Love is discovered in every act of God, even those appearing harsh. The Lord removed the first couple from the Garden of Eden after eating forbidden fruit, lovingly barring them from eating off of the tree of life and experiencing eternal selfishness and shame. (Genesis 3)

The Lord exposed David's multiple transgressions, causing him to experience public humiliation. The king gained humility and lovingly experienced forgiveness. (2 Samuel 12)

The Lord abruptly ended the life of Ananias and Sapphira, lovingly protecting the church from deception and corruption. (Acts 5)

Every action of God, some seeming punitive and unpleasant, are expressions of love. "So we have come to know and to believe the love that God has for us. God is love, and whoever abides in love abides in God, and God abides in him. By this is love perfected..., *because as he is so also are we in this world*." (1 John 4:16-17)

Motivated by love is no safeguard from being misunderstood and unappreciated. Shortly after the Civil War ended, the great Confederate military general Robert E. Lee visited a Kentucky lady. She took him to the remains of a grand old tree in front of her house and bitterly cried that the limbs and trunk were destroyed by federal artillery. She looked to Lee for a word condemning the North, or at least a little pity. After a brief silence, Lee said, "Cut it down, dear Madam, and forget it!" Out of love, she got what she needed, a push instead of pity. Was she grateful for his loving comment? Probably not!

Are there people today hoping for pity but needing a push? They may not appreciate this expression of love.

Four *walk* statements have been mentioned since entering the last half of the letter: Walk in a worthy manner (4:1), no longer *walk* as the Gentiles do (4:17), *walk* in love (5:1), and *walk* as children of light (5:8). They are interconnected, especially *walking in love* and *walking in the light*.

Followers of Jesus are to live in His love, act out of His love and display the light of His love to others. "For at one time you were darkness, but now you are light in the Lord." (V.8) A life of love manifests the light of grace living.

Unloving acts of darkness

Gaining clearer understandings of some values is often accomplished by knowing the opposite. Living in light is partially discovered by describing darkness. Paul provides a list of unloving acts, deeds directly connected to divine reprimand. Some involve conduct, others involve communication.

Three unloving actions are mentioned:

Sexual immorality! When this letter was written sexual promiscuity was readily accepted as standard behavior. Similarly, many authors and scriptwriters today make all forms of sexual activity appear as nothing more than normal instinct.

Television sitcoms have downgraded the activity of intimacy; no longer stated as *making love* but *having sex*. People are just fulfilling a bodily function. Honorable love is rarely attached to sexual behavior anymore.

Sexual immorality is a very unloving act, showing little regard for personal well-being or for the sex partner. The other person is not treated with the dignity duly merited as a child of God. They are seen as a toy for pleasure. Concern is also not shown for the present or future marriage companion, the vow of keeping oneself only for them is forever lost.

Often when people are caught in immoral sex, they are more *embarrassed* than *remorseful*; choosing cultural norms instead of Scriptural values and refusing to recognize the wrongness of such behavior. Paul reveals sexual immorality lacks the means to walk in love.

All impurity! The term impurity addresses more than sexual conduct. Moral failure is not just a sexual indiscretion but is also a violation of integrity. People restored to wholeness in Christ have their life put together, everything working harmoniously. In other words, the person has nothing to hide. He or she possesses a singleness of heart, mind, and will. Impurity, however, causes a digression away from integrity. Impurity diminishes the ability to walk in love.

Covetousness! Coveting is the unhealthy appetite to get your hands on things that belong to other people. The position or possession does not *belong* to you yet it does not *stop* you. Greed takes away the wherewithal to walk in love.

Three unloving forms of talking are also highlighted:

No filthiness, conveying "filthy language!" Presently, this manner of speaking is rampant and widespread, spilling over onto the covenant-community.

When providing leadership at a Bible College, the Dean of Students' office was located right next to mine. On one occasion, a distress signal was sent to me. I quickly went to investigate. A student was called to the office to discuss a situation and he physically threatened the administrator. His mouth was a sewer of filth, giving validity of his ability to carry out his threat, the capability to commit an unloving act. He was immediately sent back to his hometown.

Afterward, I retrieved his school records and reviewed his application. He indicated he was a committed Christian. His pastor even recommended him for admission. His language, however, indicated someone still living in darkness.

Foolish talk, conveying "empty head," another way of saying prideful or vain speaking. This kind of speech promotes selfishness, revealing a failure to recognize the reality and supremacy of God. Only a fool says in their heart, "There is no God." (Psalms 14:1)

Crude joking! Many current-day standup comedians have grown lazy in their profession. They lack the talent of earlier entertainers. They lazily try to gain laughter simply by using coarse humor. A master jokester finds wholesome ways to gain a *good* laugh.

The grammatical structure of the original language commands believers to *stop* doing or even partnering with those behaving in such ways. (V.7) Paul is not commanding them to *refrain from starting* but to *end the practice*. This type of mannerism may have been part of the past but should never be a component of the present.

The listed deeds of darkness should only be seen in people lacking faith in God, still without the resources to walk in love. These deeds are not to be associated with anyone abiding in the light of grace living. A clear *contrast* must be seen between what use to be and what now exist.

The *loving* acts of light

Living in the light is expressed by a thankful lifestyle. After listing six unloving elements of darkness, believers are instructed to have a life established by thanksgiving. (V.4)

When walking in the valley of sorrow be thankful for God's embrace, when walking on the plain of normalcy be thankful for God's company, and when walking on the mountain of joy be thankful for God's blessing. Expressions of thanksgiving are the fruit of light.

Grace living develops three great expressions of gratefulness:

Goodness: a generosity of service! The gospel writers record Jesus going about doing good. This quality is *brought to life* under the glow of grace living.

Righteousness! The early Greeks scholars defined this attribute as *giving to men and to God their due*: doing what is right. living right, and acting out of a sense of rightness. The quality is *develop*ed by the radiance of divine illumination.

Truth! Truth is best measured by *that which conforms to reality*. liberating the soul to live in authenticity. The quality *grows* by the glimmering grace of heavenly glory.

A thankful lifestyle of goodness. righteousness. and truth. the products of light. defines those walking in the love of God.

Turn on the light

Followers of Jesus have two basic obligations with regards to sin: Have nothing to do with it and expose it. How is sin revealed? By turning on the light of God in a world of darkness!

As a young boy, I was afraid of the dark. My mother often left the hall light on until I was asleep. Occasionally, I woke up in the middle of the night, after the hall light was turned off. Normal pieces of furniture made strange shadows in the dark, providing a false fantasy of reality. Once the morning light came the frightening images disappeared.

The world is living with only an illusion of reality. Most people perceive sin as pleasurable. Surrounded by deception, they think pride and rebellion will lead to fulfillment and satisfaction. Yet sin when clearly exposed is destructive. (Romans 1:18-32)

In an old black and white movie, a group of survivors was drifting aimlessly for several days on the ocean in a lifeboat. As the sun was bearing down on them, the survivors grew increasingly thirsty. In the middle of the night, while others slept, one individual surreptitiously gulped down seawater, eventually experiencing delirium and death.

Ocean water contains seven times more salt than the human body can safely ingest. The kidneys demand extra water to flush the overload of salt. The more salt water someone drinks, the thirstier they become and die of thirst.

Sin is the same way. People without faith in God thirst desperately for something harmful that looks like a solution, not realizing sin is the precise opposite of what is needed and, in fact, eventually kills.

Instead of acting and speaking out of the realm of darkness, live a life of love by living in the light. Establish a thankful heart and take on the three grace living assets of integrity, morality, and authenticity. Reveal to others the destructive force of sin by showing the life-changing force of love.

Grace living *excludes* past actions and manners of speaking and *includes* a thankful lifestyle that radiates goodness, righteousness, and truth. Turn the light on!

CHAPTER FOURTEEN

CUTTING EDGE

Look carefully then how you walk, not as unwise but as wise, making the best use of the time, because the days are evil. Therefore do not be foolish, but understand what the will of the Lord is. And do not get drunk with wine, for that is debauchery, but be filled with the Spirit, addressing one another in psalms and hymns and spiritual songs, singing and making melody to the Lord with your heart, giving thanks always and for everything to God the Father in the name of our Lord Jesus Christ. (Ephesians 5:15-20)

Paul wrote to a group of believers about the blessing of the covenant-community. She is described in the first half of his letter as a *body* having members contributing to the whole and as a *temple* giving honor to God in every aspect of life. In the last half, he gives guidelines for grace living: Individual *lifestyle* is comprised of humility, patience, and forbearance; community *unity* is held together by commonality; and, uniform *standards* are based on what Jesus did.

Living with standards includes *tensions*, requiring continual reliance on the Holy Spirit, and *contrast*, recognizing previous mannerisms no longer ruling present values. Paul now expresses a *warning*, contained in the fifth and final *walk* statement: *Look carefully how you walk!* (V. 15)

All the *walk* statements, seen together, provide a complete picture of grace living. "Walk in a manner worthy of the calling (4:1) ...no longer walk as the Gentiles do (4:17) ...walk in love (5:2) ...walk as children of light (5:8) ...look carefully then how you walk (5:15)."

The concept of *looking carefully* in the Greek means to examine with *exactness*, similar to an *edge* sharpened to precision or a *point* tapered to a perfect tip. In present day vernacular, the term *cutting edge* communicates the idea. The final *walk* pronouncement instructs believers to accurately and diligently show how grace is lived.

When growing up, I was a part of the Cub Scout program. The Den Leader repeatedly taught the Pack that the most dangerous knife is a dull knife. Why? People become *careless* instead of acting *carefully* when using a blunt instrument.

How does this apply to grace living? When faith becomes dull, love loses sharpness, and hope becomes pointless, a follower of Jesus ends up acting carelessly and living dangerously.

Two careless acts show when someone is in danger of harming themselves and failing to be a cutting edge follower of Jesus.

Not making the best use of time (V.16)

When a follower of Jesus is not looking carefully at their time, evil robs opportunities. Believers are to *utilize* rather than just *occupy* the allotted period God has established for their life.

In January 1986 my father died in the middle of the night at an RV campground near Grants Pass, Oregon. He died quickly and unexpectedly. My wife and I flew from South Dakota to Seattle for the funeral. Afterward, I told my mother I would return in six months to help remove any unwanted items.

The following summer, I returned and took a few moments to view his grave marker at the cemetery. I was struck with the cold reality that a seventy-one-year lifespan was summed up with a dash mark between two dates. Everyone is to make the most out of the *dash mark* that will ultimately define them.

Problems more readily arise when someone does not make the best use of time. They either get themselves in trouble or cause unnecessary trouble for others.

"Besides that, they learn to be idlers, going about from house to house, and not only idlers, but also gossips and busybodies, saying what they should not." (1 Timothy 5:13)

"But we urge you, brothers, to do this more and more, and to aspire to live quietly, and to mind your own affairs, and to work with your hands, as we instructed you, so that you may walk properly before outsiders and be dependent on no one." (1 Thessalonians 4:10-12)

"For even when we were with you, we would give you this command: If anyone is not willing to work, let him not eat. For we hear that some among you walk in idleness, not busy at work, but busybodies." (2 Thessalonians 3:10-11)

A classic statement still rings true, "Idle hands are the devil's workshop." Evil days are most effective when people are wasteful with time.

How should a follower of Jesus capitalize on opportunities? What are the things that actually matter? What items should have the highest priority on the *to-do* list?

Moments should be measured from an eternal perspective more than from a temporal standpoint. The best use of time involves enhancing a relationship with God and telling the world about Jesus, turning days of evil into days of grace.

Spend time developing a meaningful relationship with God. The author of time is worthy of more than just *marginal* moments. Cutting-edge living is not trivial in spiritual pursuits. Jesus gives life abundantly, the fullest use of time. What sort of attention are you giving to Him?

Spend time with family. Family time should guide life decisions. While overseeing a Bible College the Board of Regents decided advanced accreditation required a reconfiguration of the administrative structure. Part of reorganizing included the President becoming Chancellor and someone else serving as President. Since I served as the Executive Vice President, the Board invited me to become the next top administrator. I asked them to perform due diligence about the leadership needs of the institution, giving me time to carefully consider my own divine purpose and calling.

Afterward, the offer was once again extended to me yet I declined. The reason had nothing to do with doubt about individual ability, administrative skill, or personnel structure. The decision was based on having adequate time for the family. Accepting the assignment required long hours away from home and would have greatly increased the risk of my young children not receiving suitable attention from their father. Every child is parented, if not by mom and dad then by someone or something else, usually less loving and devoted.

Spend time in worthwhile activities. Your line of work, occupation, profession, or career should give testimony as done to the Lord in an expression of worship. (Colossians 3:17) By possessing divinely given talents and abilities, your endeavors should benefit others, provide for the home, and supply resources for telling His story to the nations.

Spend time in Kingdom advancement. Everyone has

a ministry. Some do kingdom activities only as long as there are individual benefits. They stay involved in church infant or children programs as long as their child participates. A few selfishly expect someone else to do ministry to their family without giving personal aid and assistance.

Throughout a lifetime, believers have a ministry to do. Sometimes the focus may prayerfully change. Yet a follower of Jesus should always be active in some measurable way.

Spend time influencing others with truth and righteousness. A well-known phrase reads, "All it takes for evil to triumph is for good people to do nothing." You are the moral compass of society, a heavenward direction arrow. Your assignment is not *isolation* but the *infiltration* and *saturation* of society with grace living. Earning the right to speak and be heard involves providing love and care to those in your world of influence, your neighbors and co-workers.

Regularly give attention to these questions: "Is mediocrity causing me to miss a *burning bush* moment with God? Are all my present activities essential and showing the best use of time?"

If not *looking carefully,* an evil age will clandestinely rob you of valuable occasions of generosity.

Failing to understand the will of the Lord (V.17)

The complete subject of God's plan is larger than can

be written in a brief letter. Paul gives attention to only one aspect, involving the inner person. God's design for the *heart* is three dimensional.

God wants you to have a Spirit-filled heart. (V.18) Paul writes, "Do not get *drunk* on wine ... be *filled* with the Spirit." *Drunk* and *filled* are not similar concepts in the original language; they are the exact opposite. He is not comparing but rather contrasting. The phrase, "drunk in the Spirit" is an oxymoron.

Drunkenness is a carnal experience, not a divine phenomenon; a deed of the flesh instead of a fruit of the Spirit. (Galatians 5:16-24) A *drunk* person is momentarily *out-of-control*; a *Spirit-filled* person expresses continual *self-control*. Instead of being *drunk* outwardly, be *filled* inwardly.

God wants you to have a melodious heart. (V.19) Manifest a divine melody from deep within your soul. Currently, music is frequently seen emanating from earbuds attached to personal electronic devices. A lack of music within the heart often necessitates carrying a tune in the pocket.

Heavenly music comes from and is offered to God. A merry heart should be customary in grace living. Let the abundance of heavenly harmony abide in your inner being. Every note and stanza of His song is divinely arranged and composed, just waiting to give a concert within you. Listen with the inner ear to the rescuing and restoring music of salvation.

God wants you to have a thankful heart. (V.20) In all his letters, Paul continually instructs thanksgiving. Why? A perpetually grateful heart minimizes discouragement and defeat.

A razor sharp existence

Cutting-edge believers are *careful* how they live. Instead of being dull and pointless, they make the most of every outward opportunity and embrace God's ultimate design for inward strength and beauty.

Steve Green sang with Bill and Gloria Gaither for six years. The Gaithers prefer performing concerts-in-the-round, requiring extra labor by the individuals rigging the necessary speakers and spotlights. *Riggers* walk the four-inch rafter beams, often a hundred feet above the concrete floor.

Green asked a member of the crew if looking down from great heights made them nervous. He was told that jobs in buildings with false ceilings, those having acoustical tiles slung a couple feet below the rafters, made them more uneasy. Workers were just as high in the air but they would sometimes believe an illusion of safety and act carelessly. The tiles could not save them if they slipped and their weight would smash them right through the flimsy ceiling.

Satan's business is not so much scaring believers to death. His business is persuading them that the danger is minimal.

Paul clearly warns that current circumstances and situations are mostly evil and can easily cause believers to stumble. Do not be foolish! Make the best use of time and possess a Spirit-filled, melodious, and thankful heart.

CHAPTER FIFTEEN

HOME

Submitting to one another out of reverence for Christ. Wives, submit to your own husbands, as to the Lord. For the husband is the head of the wife even as Christ is the head of the church, his body, and is himself its Savior. Now as the church submits to Christ, so also wives should submit in everything to their husbands. Husbands, love your wives, as Christ loved the church and gave himself up for her, that he might sanctify her, having cleansed her by the washing of water with the word, so that he might present the church to himself in splendor, without spot or wrinkle or any such thing, that she might be holy and without blemish. In the same way husbands should love their wives as their own bodies. He who loves his wife loves himself. For no one ever hated his own flesh, but nourishes and cherishes it, just as Christ does the church, because we are members of his body. "Therefore a man shall leave his father and mother and hold fast to his wife, and the two shall become one flesh." This mystery is profound, and I am saying that it refers to Christ and the church. However, let each one of you love his wife as himself, and let the wife see that she respects her husband. Children, obey your parents in the Lord, for this is right. "Honor your father and mother" (this is the first commandment with a promise), "that it may go well with you and that you may live long in the land." Fathers, do not provoke your children to anger, but bring them up in the discipline and instruction of the Lord. (Ephesians 5:21-6:4)

Wives, submit to your husbands, as is fitting in the Lord. Husbands, love your wives, and do not be harsh with them. Children, obey your parents in everything, for this pleases the Lord. Fathers, do not provoke your children, lest they become discouraged. (Colossians 3:18-21)

The family unit is in crisis today. Sociologists are redefining both marriage and household. The covenant relationship between a man and woman, with children following, is now considered too limiting and restricting of a portrayal. Marriage vows are increasingly trivialized and thought unnecessary. Heterosexual and homosexual relationships are thought inconsequential. Yet with the loss of the conventional home, there is greater evidence of dysfunction expanding and violence broadening.

Jesus prayed for His disciples, "For they are not of the world...My prayer is not that you take them out of the world...I have sent them into the world." (John 17) Followers of Jesus live *with* people embracing loose standards but dare not live *like* them. They must withstand the unpleasant pressures of this age and produce decent outcomes of behavior.

When a society embraces corrupt moorings for the home, the *new normal* works against harmonious connections and beneficial relationships. Paul's letter presents an understandable depiction of the covenant-community with a complementary illustration of the covenant-home. What qualities lend themselves to a satisfying marriage and nurturing family?

To the wife: *voluntary submission*

Whenever I was asked to perform a wedding ceremony, several pre-marital sessions were scheduled, involving hearing the couple's history, administering an analysis of their relationship, conducting a Bible study on marriage, and designing the wedding ceremony. While reviewing the responses to the Bible study, I often illustrated marriage using the two-headed monsters in older Japanese-made movies. These monsters were freaks and always ended up dead. The same is true of two-headed homes.

Most wives struggle with submission on account of the way the term is errantly defined. *Submission* does *not* mean *surrender*. The two ideas are poles apart from each other.

World War II ended with the unconditional surrender of Japan. Dropping an atomic bomb *forced* them to concede to all the conditions of the Allied Forces. If they wanted to prevent further destruction they had no choice.

The motivation behind their *surrender* was *fear*.

Scripture, however, challenges wives to submit to their husbands. *Submission* is a *voluntary* expression rooted in *love*, not fear. With deep-seated love and affection, they *willingly* yield responsibility to the husband in the marriage union. Husbands take responsibility and liability while wives establish agreement and unity.

In *surrender* people *must* give up; in *submission*, they *choose* to yield. Wives are equal with husbands yet, out of love, defer headship to him. She fulfills the precious role of the primary counselor in the decision-making process, giving priceless and paramount perspectives that afford the home higher levels of success.

In an office reception area, I was glancing at various captions in a magazine while waiting for an appointment. An unexpected statement got my attention, "Behind every successful man there is either a kind woman or a nag!" The author referred to a *nag* as a *continual drip*, like a leaky faucet pounding all night long on the ears. Nagging sometimes serves as a negative motivator: "I'll show her she's all wrong!"

The author wrote, "Abraham Lincoln died a slow death long before Booth pulled the trigger to shoot the President. Almost for a quarter of a century his wife nagged and harassed the life out of the man. She was always complaining, always criticizing her husband. Lincoln could do nothing right in her eyes.... Perhaps it was his wife's imposed limitations on him that caused him to excel." Wives will *better* help the home by giving loving counsel and edifying comments.

The term *head* means the husband is to provide spiritual leadership of the home. (V.23) If the man fails to serve as the *priestly mentor*, he abdicates his role and jeopardizes the sanctity of his family.

A wife is not expected to yield to indecent and inappropriate demands from her husband, which can be extremely challenging if married to an unbeliever. To minimize personal stress and marital strain, the union is best accomplished between two devoted followers of Jesus. Being *unequally yoked* (2 Corinthians 6:14) makes contentment and satisfaction extremely difficult to achieve.

Some women place limitations on the concept of submission: "I'll be submissive *when* my husband starts loving me." Others scathingly throw into the face of their spouse, "The Bible says you have to love me!" (V.25), an admonishment not belonging to her. If a wife no longer senses the love of her husband, how submissive is she toward him? (V.22)

The only person anyone can change is themselves. A change in attitude alters behavior and impacts the response. Wives are to base submissiveness as unto the Lord, not on the actions of their husband!

To the husband: *unconditional love*

Jesus does not bully the church and husbands should not browbeat their wife. Scripture uses terms such as *patient* and *understanding* when describing a husband toward their mate. Men and women are equal but not the same. Husbands should not expect the wife to think in similar patterns.

If Jesus treated the church like some husbands do their wives, the church would have left Him long ago. A woman is a priceless treasure of equal worth before God. For a husband to regard her as *property* damages her, as well as him.

The process of marriage is *leaving, cleaving and weaving: leave* the childhood home, *cleave* to each other (accepting instead of reforming), and become experientially *woven* into one masterpiece. When *woven* together, considering the spouse as inferior damages the *fabric* of the marriage.

When the *unconditional love* of the husband is balanced with the *voluntary submission* of the wife, the marriage flows harmoniously. An element of comfortableness develops in the relationship. The outlook of each other compliments both of them.

Husbands make a mistake by threatening, "I'll be loving *when* my wife is submissive." Some cynically throw into the face of their spouse, "The Bible says you have to be submissive!" (V.22), taking hold of the wrong phrase. If a husband no longer senses the support of his wife, how loving is he toward her? (V.25)

The only person anyone can change is themselves. A change in attitude alters behavior and impacts the response. Husbands are to base love as unto the Lord, not on the actions of the wife!

To the child: *faithful obedience*

Not everything in the home is an *entitlement* for a child. Most things are a *privilege*. Privileges are based solely on behavior. Some kids regularly abuse liberties and wrongly expect freedoms, benefits, and pleasures to continue.

The *rights* of the home include adequate lodging, nutritional meals, modest clothing, and basic education. Everything else is built on performance; such as driving a vehicle, attending events, gathering with friends, staying out late, and participating in activities. When a child refuses to obey, a parent naturally questions credibility.

Trust must be earned. When a child whines, "My parents never let me do anything," the question is, "What have you done to make them distrust you? Where in your life are you disobeying?" *Adulthood* is not measured by stature or years but determined by the exercise of *self-restraint*.

In every child's life will come a moment when parents are considered out of touch with reality. Yet somewhere between the age of 18 and 21, parents amazingly become smarter. Guess who changed?

Children occasionally consider their situation unfair. some of these feelings being justified. Who said life is fair? Children are to learn from every perceived injustice. They have the parents they have and nothing changes this reality. A child is to learn from both their *counsel* and *mistakes*.

My father died when I was 36 years old. In the entire time we journeyed life together. not once did he ever say. "I love you!" It bothered me immensely, well into my 20's. Some therapist would classify this as traumatic and damaging. Hogwash! He never said the words but demonstrated love in numerous ways. I learned from his lack of spoken affirmation and daily expressed love to my own children.

Young people occasionally threaten, "I'll be obedient *when* Mom and Dad stop annoying me." Some have scornfully said to their parent, "You're not supposed to make me angry or cause me to become embittered!" (V.2). highlighting the wrong phrase. If a child no longer senses parental support. how obedient are they toward them? (V.1)

The only person anyone can change is themselves. A change in attitude alters behavior and impacts the response. Children are to base obedience as unto the Lord. not on the actions of the parents!

To the parent: *patient discipline*

A fuzzy line exists between demanding too much and expecting too little. Demand too *much* and a child can feel overwhelmed; expect too *little* and the parent loses respect. Too *small* of a demand and a child remains dependent; too *big* of an expectation and a child loses courage.

The patient discipline of children is both *fair* and *firm*. Standards should be reachable but high. Obedience should be obtainable yet challenging. They may be young but a child is simply a person in a smaller body. If you do not *stretch* them as a child, they will *snap* as an adult.

Children deserve to be parented by understanding moms and dads. Harassing often causes a child to question expectations. Constantly pushing can lead to perpetual resistance. Children need to respond to instructions but this is best accomplished by outthinking them. The adult has the more developed brain and should creatively exercise the gray-matter.

Parents have been known to threaten, "I'll be less demanding *when* my child obeys me." Some with exasperation have said to their children, "You're supposed to obey me!" (V.1), emphasizing the wrong phrase. If a mom and dad are not sensing a child's obedience, how patiently disciplining are they with them? (V.4)

The only person anyone can change is themselves. A change in attitude alters behavior and impacts the response. Parents are to render patient disciplining as unto the Lord, not on the actions of the child!

Home life

Paul does not mention every aspect of marriage and family in his letter. What he does write is for wives to voluntarily submit, husbands to unconditionally love, children to faithfully obey, and parents to patiently discipline. The common denominator for each household member to embrace is grace.

Has peer pressure and political correctness caused some to embrace rebellious viewpoints instead of upholding the clear instruction of Scripture? Unfortunately, yes! Opinions rooted in defiance need to change. Outlooks can be transformed by grace, producing a brighter future for each person in the covenant-home.

Grace living among family members is all about love; a wife loving submissively, a husband loving unconditionally, children loving obediently, and parents loving patiently.

CHAPTER SIXTEEN

WORK

Bondservants, obey your earthly masters with fear and trembling, with a sincere heart, as you would Christ, not by the way of eye-service, as people-pleasers, but as bondservants of Christ, doing the will of God from the heart, rendering service with a good will as to the Lord and not to man, knowing that whatever good anyone does, this he will receive back from the Lord, whether he is a bondservant or is free. Masters, do the same to them, and stop your threatening, knowing that he who is both their Master and yours is in heaven, and that there is no partiality with him. (Ephesians 6:5-9)

Two locations consume most of everyone's waking moments, house and workplace. Combined together they take up the majority of the weekly agenda. Family and occupation are the two leading areas for showing Jesus to others. Home life and work ethic are to give testimony of grace living. After writing about the family, Paul addresses labor conditions.

The subject of employment in this letter gives attention to master/slave relations. Paul is not condoning slavery, only acknowledging its existence. One estimate indicates approximately 60 million people, one-third of the Roman Empire population, were slaves at the time. Paul shows how to divinely make harmonious connections out of unfortunate practices. Comparisons can be made between a slave/master and an employee/employer connection.

The book <u>Why America Doesn't Work</u> describes disintegrating families, crime-ridden streets, and economic chaos. Part of the problem is workers seemingly wanting to produce less yet benefit more. The author concludes things are not working well in the United States.

North America possesses an abundance of natural resources and individual resourcefulness, yet fewer Americans are content in their career. Surveys reveal, while having every advantage, the very thing making the country great is in trouble. Most do not want to work hard and are losing the significance and importance of labor. The economic engine is running down.

For better or worse employment defines people. In a sense, people work, therefore they are. The question, "What do you do?" is usually the first question asked when meeting someone.

Work is one of the few constants of life, one of the

few common factors of humanity. A job is much more than a need to keep busy or bring home income. Noteworthy employment is fundamental to human existence, an expression of a person's very nature.

Paul gave attention to the tenets of work by writing to believers, "Now we command you, brothers, in the name of our Lord Jesus Christ, that you keep away from any brother who is walking in idleness and not in accord with the tradition that you received from us. For you yourselves know how you ought to imitate us, because we were not idle when we were with you, nor did we eat anyone's bread without paying for it, but with toil and labor we worked night and day, that we might not be a burden to any of you. It was not because we do not have that right, but to give you in ourselves an example to imitate. For even when we were with you, we would give you this command: If anyone is not willing to work, let him not eat. For we hear that some among you walk in idleness, not busy at work, but busybodies. Now such persons we command and encourage in the Lord Jesus Christ to do their work quietly and to earn their own living. As for you, brothers, do not grow weary in doing good. If anyone does not obey what we say in this letter, take note of that person, and have nothing to do with him, that he may be ashamed. Do not regard him as an enemy, but warn him as a brother." (2 Thessalonians 3:6-15)

Two rules should determine the actions of a believer in their career: they are duty-bound to *not* use spiritual freedom as an excuse for unfaithful service, and they are obligated to do a job to the best of their ability.

Work as servants of Christ (V.5)

Paul makes mention of "eye service," (V.6) literally *when eyes are on you.* Some people only make an effort when someone they want to impress is present. Yet Jesus is always cognizant of what His followers are doing.

A major form of thievery occurring on the job is stealing of *time*: idly sitting at a desk, unnecessary visits with co-workers, private phone calls during business hours, and doing personal matters on company errands. These actions steal productivity and impact profit.

Another form of disservice to a company is talking to others about salvation instead of working. Believers are to be a witness but their greatest testimony in the workplace is job performance. A quote of Francis of Assisi slightly modified may apply in these situations: Witness all the time, use words when *appropriate.*

Christian organizations occasionally attract both naïve and unscrupulous workers, thinking the business is a *perfect* work environment or an *easy rip-off*. Neither is true!

Unfortunately, institutions devoted to compassion and benevolence have hired people acknowledging Christ that end up taking advantage of the organization's core values, behaving like leeches and sucking dry limited resources. If dealt with justly, management is sometimes accused of acting unchristian. Yet the shady and sneaky worker is actually a *thief in the temple*, confronted and stopped from doing more disgraceful actions.

The Carpenter from Nazareth performed manual labor and His followers were hard-working people, many rising before dawn to drag smelly fishing nets. The community of believers was birthed by the working class, striving tirelessly out of love for God as *fishers of men*. Faith in God is a laborer's faith.

Work wholeheartedly (V.7)

Many employees attempt to do the bare minimum, just enough to get by. Those loving Jesus should *avoid* this temptation and give maximum effort; in other words, *go for the max*.

In older generations, the expression *company man* was a badge of distinction. My grandfather was a train conductor with the Great Northern railroad for over 50 years, receiving a gold watch upon retirement. My father was a train engineer for 43 years, retiring at the highest ranking and with several distinctions.

They were both perceived as company men, helping make the rail industry more safe and successful. Yet today, with the outgrowth of constant career changes, a loyalty to company goals has diminished, causing corporations to fail achieving their objectives.

For followers of Jesus, drive and ambition are directly linked to the Lord. When the workday is over, they should ask themselves, "Would Jesus be pleased with my job performance? Would the Lord be thrilled to call my work His own?"

With the global escalation of the *entitlement* mentality, many people carry a chip on their shoulder. an unwholesome attitude. Some complain about employers: others treat customers as an inconvenience. Thinking poorly about bosses or patrons are unsavory characteristics.

Grumbling about wages and benefits should be shunned by those devoted to Christ. Guard your heart and measure the meaning of employment by the standards of grace living.

The intangible (V.8)

Corporate surveys reveal good wages is not the primary goal of employment. Statistics indicate primary goals are contentment, interest, satisfaction, and fulfillment. Happiness is more than earnings. Labor Unions normally cannot negotiate *intangible* benefits.

A rich industrialist was disturbed to find a fisherman sitting lazily beside his boat. "Why aren't you out fishing?" he asked. The fisherman replied, "Because I've caught enough fish for today."

"Why don't you catch more fish than you need?" the rich man wondered. The fisherman responded, "What would I do with them?"

"You could earn more money, buy a better boat and go deeper out on the waters to catch more fish," he said impatiently. "You could purchase nylon nets, catch even more fish, and make more money. Soon you'd have a fleet of boats and be rich like me."

The fisherman asked, "Then what would I do?" The industrialist said, "You could sit down and enjoy life."

"What do you think I'm doing now?" came the reply. The rich man forgot that work is the *source* of happiness, not the *road* to happiness.

People have been known to decline perceived promotions, a few even promising more financial security. Why? Because most of life is spent working! Everyone should do something they find personally interesting, fulfilling, and meaningful.

Do what the Lord has designed for your life, without concern of lavish and lush provisions. The most enjoyable dimension of life cannot be purchased with money.

A word to employers (V.9)

Paul made a few comments to those providing jobs.

Treat workers as you want to be treated. Employers are only as good as the people employed by them and eventually become a reflection of the boss. Everyone puts on their shoes the same way, one foot at a time. Regard them with dignity. Show them courtesy and respect.

Allow room for self-expression. Why hire someone similar to yourself and limit the outcomes to merely your capabilities? Why employ someone only to forbid them from expressing their personality and creativity to the fullest potential? When uniquely gifted and talented employees take personal ownership of an assignment, they make the boss and business more successful.

If a worker's personality is offensive or their creativity is weak, you are showing something about yourself: You have poor hiring skills. Either learn from your mistakes or give the task to someone more capable.

Is employing someone distinctly different than you a risk? Absolutely! But when has achieving a higher level of success ever come without an element of danger? Get over yourself and watch the company flourish.

Avoid threatening employees. Intimidation does not achieve better performance. Fear of losing employment does not accomplish desired results. An overly demanding and exacting boss will frustrate otherwise fantastic workers.

During Air Force Basic Training the drill instructors had two volumes, loud or silent. Every order was yelled and performance was never good enough. Some Airman lost heart, believing every task was impossible for them to reach or what they did was unimportant. Threatening caused low morale, producing an increase of diminished performance and eventually forming indifference.

If someone cannot do the work, after thorough instructions and careful guidance, be merciful and dismiss them. A worker cannot gain a sense of satisfaction if they are unable to meet job expectations.

Remember that everyone is equal before God. In Christ, employees and employers are servants of the same Lord. There are no distinctions before the Heavenly Father. Workers on earth are also heavenly family members. Treat them graciously.

Work

The best employers and employees of any organization should be those following Jesus. They should be both exceptional leaders and faithful workers. God established the work ethos at creation, laboring for six days and resting on the seventh. When Jesus is Lord, He restores His image in people living by grace, which includes excellent labor habits.

Someday, when standing before the Lord, there will be no hiding actual behavior. He alone knows if what was done is honorable. He alone knows the attitude and motives behind every action. He alone gives accurate rewards for actual efforts. A job is part of grace living, done as unto the Lord.

CHAPTER SEVENTEEN

ARMOR

Finally, be strong in the Lord and in the strength of his might. Put on the whole armor of God, that you may be able to stand against the schemes of the devil. For we do not wrestle against flesh and blood, but against the rulers, against the authorities, against the cosmic powers over this present darkness, against the spiritual forces of evil in the heavenly places. Therefore take up the whole armor of God, that you may be able to withstand in the evil day, and having done all, to stand firm. Stand therefore, having fastened on the belt of truth, and having put on the breastplate of righteousness, and, as shoes for your feet, having put on the readiness given by the gospel of peace. In all circumstances take up the shield of faith, with which you can extinguish all the flaming darts of the evil one; and take the helmet of salvation, and the sword of the Spirit, which is the word of God. (Ephesians 6:10-17)

For though we walk in the flesh, we are not waging war

according to the flesh. For the weapons of our warfare are not of the flesh but have divine power to destroy strongholds. We destroy arguments and every lofty opinion raised against the knowledge of God, and take every thought captive to obey Christ. (2 Corinthians 10:3-5)

The first part of Paul's letter explains the specially created church. The covenant-community is comprised of divinely called leaders and devoted followers of Jesus. She *operates* as a body and a temple, *functions* in unity, and *reflects* purity.

The last part of the letter describes how following Jesus is carried out: namely, living by grace. Paul creates a few soliloquies of grace living as seen in *gatherings*, *home*, and *work*. He then transitions to show grace living as a *battle* against evil strongholds.

A difficult and dangerous conflict is currently taking place. No believer is exempt from enemy assaults, nor can anyone sit idly by and do nothing. Instead, they are exhorted to be alert and to endure. Paul writes, "...able to stand ...stand firm ...stand therefore."

While imprisoned, with Roman guards close by, Paul uses the military uniform as a vivid portrayal of preparedness. The armament mentioned mainly provides protection while fighting. The bulk of the equipment is for *holding ground*. Yet Matthew records Jesus telling His disciples that the church is *advancing* and beating down the entryway of evil. While the covenant-community aggressively presses onward, the gates of Hell are unable to hold up against the overwhelming force of the Holy Spirit. (Matthew 16:18-19)

Both holding ground (defense) and advancement (offense) are critical for winning the battle against cosmic powers and spiritual forces. The Army of the Lord must *secure* gained territory as well as *claim* new ones. The question is: As believers advance are they giving up regions once made righteous in Christ?

An eighty-six-year-old retired insurance broker concluded the existence of a personal God and life after death cannot be true. He based his speculation on the lack of Christlikeness among those claiming to love God. He considered believers just as greedy, dishonest, unkind, ungrateful, and discontented as unbelievers. He felt they simply added admiration for a Supreme Being to a list of poor actions and revolting mannerisms.

The way some people live gives an opportunity for others to slander the Lord. The lifestyle of *some* is calling into question the character of *everyone* living in grace. Paul extends a challenge to all those following Jesus to *draw a line in the sand* and say, "Enough! No more can people call into question the majesty of God and the purity of grace by my behavior."

With a resolve to lift up Christ, believers are not left helpless in the battle against corruption, both defensively and offensively. They have been given the armor of God and the sword of the Spirit. Will they put it on and use it?

Know where your *strength* lies (Vs. 10-11)

Followers of Jesus are *strong in the Lord*. (V.10) A distinction exists when Paul writes about home, work, and conflict. Marriage is done "as to the Lord." (5:22) Employment is done "as to the Lord." (6:7) But conflict is fought "in the Lord." (6:10).

No one is personally strong. The might of His strength is needed. The Lord is strong and, without Him, believers lack the means to triumph.

Luke records Satan demanding permission to sift Peter like wheat yet Jesus interceded. (Luke 22:31) Without divine intervention, believers are vulnerable and susceptible to total defeat, even loyal and confident followers like Peter.

The eternal conflict is serious and no one can afford to be self-reliant. The grammatical structure of the phrase "be strong" (V.10) is demanding *continuous dependence* upon God. Also, the phrase "put on" (V.11) demands an *action done* by a person. When facing conflict in a rebellious world, disciples are responsible to regularly get dressed with divine strength.

While serving a church in Montana, a teenager accused me of using Jesus as a crutch. Actually, everyone has a crutch. Some lean on intoxicating beverages, others depend on cancer-laden nicotine, many find comfort in excessive eating, and a few subject themselves to mind-bending chemicals. Money is another kind of crutch, often synonymous with a false sense of security.

Jesus is the only sure peg to hold onto. Attempting to face conflict without His strength ends in defeat.

Know where your *struggle* lies (Vs. 12-13)

A minister one Sunday told the congregates, "We wrestle with principalities and powers – and mean people." Humorous but not quite accurate! Conflicts are challenging because battles are not against those possessing wayward deficiencies but, instead, against unseen evil forces.

This time, Paul uses the phrase *heavenly places* to denote the murky world of darkness. Followers of Jesus are not just shadowboxing or beating the air against an imaginary foe. The unseen cosmic enemy is real.

The conflict is not against people. People may abuse believers but they are not the enemy. They may reject or rebuff followers of Jesus but they are not the ultimate problem.

Although an uncomfortable thought, unpleasant people and downright scoundrels are sometimes a source of personal refinement. With help from the Holy Spirit, anyone can become a better person because of them. Annoying and irritating people, when handled with grace, often cure believers of impatience and anger.

The conflict is also not against other believers. If the focus of conflict is *in-house*, little is needed by enemy forces to tear down. Followers of Jesus often do a good job of destroying without external influence.

No two members of any family think exactly the same. Difference of opinions are allowed. Similarly, not everything in Christ is a hard fast rule, even such things as dietary restrictions. (1 Corinthians 10). Avoid petty issues and redirect focus toward the real enemy!

The conflict is also not against human government. Paul wrote this letter in the capital city of Rome while waiting for an appeal before government officials. Impartial justice is critical for the well-being of every society and is a major purpose for civil authority. Yet public servants are never better than the believers that pray for them.

"First of all, then, I urge that supplications, prayers, intercessions, and thanksgivings be made for all people, for kings and all who are in high positions, that we may lead a peaceful and quiet life, godly and dignified in every way." (1 Timothy 2:1-2)

The conflict is against the rebellious spirit of the current age; against "powers over this present darkness," the "spiritual forces of evil," involving demonic influences, devilish schemes, and evil trickery. The archenemy of God is determined to defeat divine purposes, partly done by unseen evil forces far more subtle and cunning than often portrayed.

Failure, however, is also accomplished by the rebellious sinful nature. Some consider Deliverance Ministries as the best solution for addressing every kind of failure. Are there times when this is mistakenly applied?

If people could choose between taking responsibility for their actions or accusing another source, most would prefer to point the finger at an outside influence. When a flaw surfaces, which better minimizes a sense of personal blame?

If a person goes into a fit of rage, some mistakenly call it a *spirit* of anger ("the devil made me do it" syndrome) and sometimes seek deliverance. Yet Paul indicates fits of rage are actually *deeds of the flesh*, attached more to sin than Satan. No one is *delivered* from the flesh; they must *crucify* the flesh. "And those who belong to Christ Jesus have crucified the flesh with its passions and desires." (Galatians 5:24)

Deliverance has to do with demonic influence, not the sinful nature. Much of contemporary deliverance ministries are aimed at *flesh* problems and end up fruitless. With dependency on God, personal initiative is required to address character defects.

Know where your *safety* lies (Vs. 14-17)

Believers have all the necessary equipment for victory in the conflict against evil.

Belt of truth protects against deceit. A loose belt speaks of ease and carelessness. When a believer is firmly surrounded by truth, they cannot be snagged by trickery. Everyone is to encase themselves with authenticity.

Breastplate of righteousness protects the heart. Passions and desires covered with the righteousness of Christ prevent a soul from being *morally* wounded. Righteous living rather than verbal arguments is the most successful defense against accusations. The best way to effectively address allegations is doing what is right.

Feet fitted with readiness makes for a sure-footed journey through enemy territory. Believers are moving forward with the message of grace and hope. Each step is to be saturated with the presence of the Prince of Peace.

Shield of faith is the divine defense that mightily stops the dangerous arrows of despair. Shields move quickly to vulnerable places, providing protection against every angle of attack. No follower of Jesus can afford to be without the safety of faith, not even for a moment.

The helmet of salvation protects the command center, the wellspring of life. "But since we belong to the day, let us be sober, having put on the breastplate of faith and love, and *for a helmet the hope of salvation.*" (1 Thessalonians 5:8) If hope becomes injured, the mind loses the grace of sound reasoning, correct attitudes, and right motives.

The sword of the Spirit is the word of God, the most effective weapon for fighting. Jesus entered the wilderness of temptation and responded to every inducement of Satan with Scripture. His followers must do the same.

A rancher tried everything to stop coyotes from

killing her sheep in southern Montana. She tried odor sprays and electric fences. She slept in the field with the sheep during the summer. She placed radios near them. She corralled her herd at night. She still lost fifty head of sheep that year, until she discovered Llamas.

Llamas do not appear to be afraid of anything. When they see something, they put their head up and walk straight toward it. To a coyote, this is aggressive behavior. They will have nothing to do with it. Coyotes are opportunists and Llamas take the opportunity away.

God's word fights in comparable ways. His pronouncements take away every pervasive and plausible prospect of defeat.

Running away

Look carefully! There is no protection for the back. Followers of Jesus suffer loss against the spirit of the age and the enemy of the soul when they run from the conflict, when they desert spiritual readiness and holy resolve.

Good spiritual habits must frame grace living, such as studying Scripture, praying, joining arms with other believers, and living out an accurate testimony. These actions keep the equipment of warfare efficient and effectual. Safety is found by keeping the tools of battle in top shape.

If basic disciplines are neglected, doubt develops with regards to the strength of the heavenly armor, which may cause flight instead of fight and leave the spiritual backside exposed to the enemy. With divine instruments in good repair, ditching the conflict is never considered.

Know where your *strength* lies. Know where your *struggle* lies. Know where your *safety* lies. Your strength is in the Lord. Your struggle is with the spirit of the age. Your safety is the armor of God. Keep the armament of heaven in mint condition using good spiritual routines – then stand, stand, and stand!

CHAPTER EIGHTEEN

ALERT

Praying at all times in the Spirit, with all prayer and supplication. To that end keep alert with all perseverance, making supplication for all the saints, and also for me, that words may be given to me in opening my mouth boldly to proclaim the mystery of the gospel, for which I am an ambassador in chains, that I may declare it boldly, as I ought to speak. (Ephesians 6:18-20)

Paul previously wrote about the covenant-community in spiritual conflict and the importance of knowing about your strength, struggle, and safety. Believers are to stand firm against the enemy of the soul by leaning on Jesus, fully equipped for battle.

Alertness is as critical as equipment, elevating the importance of prayer. Vigilance gives attention to being watchful and awake instead of negligent and snoozing. The disciples were sleeping in the Garden of Gethsemane while soldiers were entering the Kidron valley. Had they been attentive and looking, they would have noticed the enemy coming and been better prepared to respond correctly. (Luke 22:47-51)

Fifteen times the New Testament gives attention to *alertness*, primarily in three realms: *mindful* of the adversary, *watchful* for the Second Coming, and *faithful* in prayer.

The devil wants to keep followers of Jesus from praying. Satan fears nothing from prayerless studies, prayerless work, and prayerless religion. He mocks at wisdom, laughs at toil, but trembles at prayer.

Besides not fully comprehending the power of prayer, many misunderstand the nature and purpose of intercession. Followers of Jesus are to actively and consistently plead for divine intervention. Entreaties are appeals coming from both *mind* and *Spirit*. Supplications are not some kind of mindless trance or repetitive chant.

Dialogue with God, the Supreme Leader, keeps the church alert while experiencing conflict with the forces of darkness. Having only ministers praying is not enough; the entire covenant-community must pray. Grace living includes everyone passionately and mightily conversing with the Lord God Almighty.

Paul highlights two words, two phrases, and two subjects that are patterns of attentive praying.

Two *words*

The first word is *prayer*. Devotedly talking to God is critical for steadiness during conflict. Out of a longing for instructions from the Commander in Chief, believers are to discuss the situation with Him respectfully and observantly.

Prayer comes out of a yearning to personally hear from God, consisting of praise, thanksgiving, discourse, listening, and rejoicing. The primary focus of prayer is not *needs* but *conversation*.

Do you have someone in your life who only talks to you when they want something? Whenever they approach do you wonder, "Now, what do they want?" Are believers doing the same with the Lord? He desires *regular* interaction with His troops, sizing up earthly weaknesses and heavenly strengths.

The second word is *supplication*, meaning to seek, ask, entreat, and petition. Believers are also encouraged to come and present the needs of the moment. God genuinely cares and desires to hear the complaints and frustrations currently taking place. He is never too busy to listen to battle concerns.

Do you have a problem? He wants to hear it! Are you afraid, aggrieved, or alarmed? He wants to render comfort! God never tires listening about the issues you are facing. He wishes to respond to all your needs.

Notice the order: "with all prayer and supplication."

(V.18) Consistently come and have a conversation, then speak about disturbing matters, as needed.

A man encountered some trouble while flying his small airplane. He called the Control Tower and said, "Pilot to tower, I'm 300 miles from the airport, six hundred feet above the ground, out of fuel, and descending rapidly. Please advise. Over!" The dispatcher replied, "Tower to pilot, repeat after me: 'Our Father, Who art in heaven....'"

A crisis is not the best time to *introduce* yourself to God. He should already be known by you. Never consider the Lord as simply a Life Preserver or Problem Solver: a readily available Panic Button activated during times of emergency. Build a relationship with Him *before* asking for help and special intervention.

Some debate whether God listens to the wants and wishes of those *not* following Jesus. One thing is certain: It is not required of Him. The chief aim of prayer is building a relationship with the Lord. When you consistently pray, talking to God about current troubles does not abuse the relationship.

Two *phrases*

The first phrase is *at all times*. Prayer is not a *posture* but, rather, an *activity*. Prayer is conversing with God as if chatting with someone right next to you. He is always present; be mindful of His presence. There is not an occasion or moment when you cannot speak with the Lord.

Communicating with someone is not always verbal. A glance, a look, a touch are forms of interfacing. Your life *at all times* should show signs of connectedness, sending a message to others that you are in constant contact with Him and He with you.

Prayer has no physical positions, no boundaries, no limitations, and no restricted locations. Kneeling is fine, prayer rooms are good, but He is always nearby. Believers can always pray.

The second phrase is *in the Spirit*. Are you abiding in the fullness of the Spirit? Is your heart fully and passionately engaged with Him? Is your inner nature filled with His holy presence, helping you to speak confidently with the Heavenly Father?

A benefit of Spirit-living is occasionally overlooked: Have you *prayed for acceptance* when Jesus has already accepted you? Have you *prayed for grace* when the Lord has already given sufficient grace? Have you *prayed for peace* when God has already given an incomprehensible peace? Have you *prayed for strength* when Scripture already declares you can do all things? These qualities are appropriated by simply abiding in Christ, and by living *in the Spirit* you gain the constant assurance of these blessings.

Regularly allow the Holy Spirit to mediate in and through you. "Likewise the Spirit helps us in our weakness. For we do not know what to pray for as we ought, but the Spirit himself intercedes for us with groanings too deep for words. And he who searches hearts knows what is the mind of the Spirit, because the Spirit intercedes for the saints according to the will of God." (Romans 8:26-27) Conversing with God should include prayers saturated by the Spirit, directed and guided by Him.

Conversations with God are to be at all times and should include Spirit praying.

Two *subjects*

The first subject is *supplication for all the saints*. Believers are to be alert, attentive, and always praying for each other. Should a follower of Jesus stumble in the battle, others should lift up the saintly warrior in prayer! One of the best ways to experience a divine sense of community is by relentlessly pursuing before the Throne the best interest of every believer.

The second subject is that *words may be given...to proclaim the mystery of the gospel*. Accurate and solid presentations of His story come from spokespersons drenched with the anointing of prayer, freshly poured over them by others.

Gaining divine direction for the covenant-community is very demanding. Regularly having an illuminating word from the Lord for others is exacting work. A thirty-minute presentation of the Way, the Truth, and the Life involves hours of prayerful preparation and an emotionally draining delivery. George Whitefield preached more than 18,000 sermons in 34 years (12,419 days), an average of 10 sermons a week. This triggers a tremendous mental and physical toll.

Most ministers talk to the same group of people each week. How do they faithfully bring interesting, meaningful, and enlightening insight about divine realities? Only when the hearers unfailingly lift up the proclaimer in prayer, making the light of truth bright and vivid for all the listeners.

If a person chooses a loose lifestyle, confronting them about improper living is naturally uncomfortable, creating moments of internal unease. What compassionate person actually looks forward to angering, insulting, or hurting someone? The older covenant prophet Jeremiah often struggled warning those already uniformly rejecting eternal values, causing a disquieted soul. Communicators need great boldness, a special ability to speak up against errant behavior. They need others to pray for them to be brave and courageous.

Those presenting the Good News desire to give a clear explanation of His word, only possible by a heavy dose of heavenly inspiration. They want to express life-changing thoughts in a way that caringly reflects the Lord. Followers of Jesus assist them by praying a fresh fire of purity on their thoughts and ambitions.

Believers are to stand in the gap and provide the link between proclaimers and hearers, petitioning the Lord for ears to hear what the Spirit is saying to the church. Cry out to God for both sincere speakers and earnest listeners.

A call to alertness

The church is at war with sin, Satan, and the spirit of the age. Followers of Jesus must be properly equipped and readily alert. They must be both *skillful* and *watchful*.

Among the joys of grace living is being continually and steadfastly in prayer, gaining greater victory and eternal triumph. A poem about a humble believer named Jim captures a beautiful benefit of prayer: (*author unknown*)

> *For years each day he'd rise to pray:*
> *And when in church, he'd bow his knee*
> *And meekly say, "Dear God, it's Jim."*
> *And when he'd leave, we all could see*
> *God's holy presence walked with him.*

> *As Jim grew old, the chastening rod*
> *Of years left him so ill and drawn.*
> *His path to church is now untrod:*
> *But in his heart each day at dawn*
> *He hears the words, "Dear Jim, it's God."*

Genuine prayer is not a burden but a glorious opportunity to talk to the One who gives guidance and strength during frightful moments.

Significant conversations with God are initiated by *you*. Prayer takes determination. Faithfully praying takes diligence. Meaningful prayers take preparation. You are to be constantly on alert – before, during, and after the conflicts that naturally occur throughout life.

Regularly report to your Supreme Commander through prayer! Ascertain His strategy, get His marching orders, and implement His plan!

CHAPTER NINETEEN

ENCOURAGEMENT

So that you also may know how I am and what I am doing, Tychicus the beloved brother and faithful minister in the Lord will tell you everything. I have sent him to you for this very purpose, that you may know how we are, and that he may encourage your hearts. (Ephesians 6:21-22)

Paul's letter to the Ephesians uncovers the mystery of the covenant-community and the nature of grace living.

The church is uniquely designed and comprised of divinely called leaders *in Christ* and devoted followers *of Christ*.

The church is like a human body, having the symmetry of oneness; where every fiber, tissue, organ, and vessel works best when in harmony with one another.

The church is a sacred temple where the holy and merciful Lord is worshiped.

The church abides in grace, a manner of living that *reflects* the love of God (Ch.4); *reveals* His nature both at home and at work (Ch.5); and *rightly* battles the various forces of darkness by standing spiritually equipped and eternally alert (Ch.6).

What helps the covenant-community fulfill her purpose and provides aid in grace living? Encouragement! The ministries of Apostles, Prophets, Evangelists, and Pastor-teachers equip believers for a life of service, which includes encouraging them to prevail. Divinely called leaders regularly reassure devoted followers of Jesus about the good progress they are making in their spiritual advancement.

A prominent minister was taking a flight to a Christian conference and planned to spend his flying time getting caught up on a few projects. An old-fashioned church revivalist happened to be assigned the seat right next to him.

When the itinerate preacher noticed the name of the minister on one of his papers, he decided to capitalize on this unexpected opportunity and share his opinion about the condition of the church. He declared, "The church is lost, hell-bound and heartsick. I wake 'em up. Christians are asleep. They don't pray. They don't love. They don't care." He then took on a classical cadence and preaching tone, listing all the woes and weaknesses of the church. "Too lazy-uh, too rich-uh, too spoiled-uh, too fat-uh...."

These types of broad generalizations do not

encourage. How does the Lord want His messengers to inspire? What message does He want said? Paul shows the ingredients of an encouraging word.

The message is *not* about destruction

How many come to a worship gathering for a fierce tongue-thrashing? When has brow-beating ever ended with heart change? Only masochists hope for and find pleasure in harsh whippings.

Those earnestly seeking to follow Jesus know their life is occasionally out of sync with God. The Holy Spirit, dwelling within, convicts and makes people aware when they act rebelliously and wrongly. No one needs to provide an abrasive tone of criticism.

Ministers serving as shepherds have a rod, yet not for beating. The shepherd's stick is never for striking and abusing the sheep. The instrument lends support and is used to guide, help, rescue, and protect. (Psalms 23)

There are times when rods are applied to the *rump* to get sheep moving in the right direction but never applied to the *back* for chastening. A shepherd, sent from God, possesses great patience and gentleness.

"And the Lord's servant must not be quarrelsome but kind to everyone, able to teach, patiently enduring evil, correcting his opponents with gentleness. God may perhaps grant them repentance leading to a knowledge of the truth." (2 Timothy 2:24-25)

"Preach the word; be ready in season and out of season; reprove, rebuke, and exhort, with complete patience and teaching." (2 Timothy 4:2)

A pastor uses the rod of grace for building, not destroying. The message is not for denunciation but elevation.

The message is the *full council* of God

The messenger is to "tell you everything," (V.21) not just what you want to hear but what you *need* to hear. There are no limitations as to the content of the message. God wants you to know His methods, meaning the manner in which He normally operates. The Lord wants you to understand how He lovingly treats those living by grace. Grasping His ways brings clarity to His handiwork.

Messengers encourage as *beloved family* members. (V.21) The term means literally *coming from the same womb*.

My sister and I were the last living members of my parents' home and loved each other very much. Our outlook on life was similar in many ways yet also quite different. She came to the conclusion God did not exist and there was no life after death. Yet, we were family. Before she died, I spoke to her about the need for a relationship with God. I did so as someone coming from the same womb, out of love instead of condemnation.

The concept *born again* carries the *same-womb* idea. Believers are members of the same family.

Encouragement is spoken with love, not like an accuser pointing out faults.

Messengers are also *faithful*. (V.21) Someone who is faithful *lives the encouraging way* before attempting to *speak encouragement*. Telling others about grace begins by modeling grace living.

"Shepherd the flock of God that is among you, exercising oversight, not under compulsion, but willingly, as God would have you; not for shameful gain, but eagerly; not domineering over those in your charge, but *being examples* to the flock." (1 Peter 5:2-3)

"Brothers, join in *imitating me*, and keep your eyes on those who walk according to *the example* you have in us." (Philippians 3:17)

Regardless the gifts and talents of an orator or how amazing the elucidation, what does their lifestyle reveal? Are business dealings honest; are conversations appropriate; are relationships honorable; are associations respectful? Do they avoid selfish pursuits; do they manifest genuine humility? What is said is often forgotten but personal actions are never overlooked or ignored.

Messengers are part of the message. The lifestyle of an emissary must be consistent with an inspiring word. A trustworthy messenger plus a message seeded with love encourages.

The message is about courage

Life is a combination of *successes* and *setbacks*. When successes are greater than setbacks, a person has courage and senses joy. If setbacks become greater than successes, discouragement soon follows.

Life is also comprised of three major components: personal, family, and professional obligations. When the setbacks are greater than the successes *in more than one area at the same time*, discouragement easily slips into *depression*.

Do followers of Jesus sometimes lose heart? Yes! And a loss of heart leads to an absence of courage. While in the grips of *discouragement*, sensing a lack of *courage*, the remedy is *encouragement*. "I have sent him to you for this very purpose...that he may encourage your heart." (V.22)

A classic song of the church is worth remembering and repeating: "No one ever cared for me like Jesus: there's no other friend so kind as He; no one else could take the sin and darkness from me – O how much He cared for me."

Colossians, a companion letter from Paul, confirms *encouragement is for the heart*. (Colossians 4:7-9) The Lord wants believers to cheer up, preventing them from losing heart. If troubled, Jesus has an uplifting word, custom designed for His followers.

Should warnings about eternal damnation stop?

Should admonishments about right-living end? These messages are important and true but should come from a loving family member, not an accusatory faultfinder. In an era of terrorism, may a messenger not act like a radical and militant terrorist.

Encouragement always resonates with faith, hope, and love, traits that usher people into an anticipation for the future. (1 Corinthians 13:12-13)

Love and care

From 1986 to 1990, Frank Reed was held hostage in a Lebanon cell. For months at a time he was blindfolded, living in complete darkness, or chained to a wall and kept in absolute silence. On one occasion he was moved to another room and although blindfolded could sense others were also present. But it was three weeks before he dared peek out and discovered he was chained next to Terry Anderson and Tom Sutherland.

Although he was beaten, made ill, and tormented, Reed suffered the most from a lack of anyone caring. During an interview, he said, "Nothing I did mattered to anyone. I began to realize how withering it is to exist with not a single expression of caring around me. I learned one overriding fact: caring is a powerful force. If no one cares, you are truly alone."

Encouragement to the covenant-community emphasizes *a divine love* that resonates with *genuine care*. A bit of prose lays out the message:

That's My Soul

That's my soul lying there;
I put it there so you could touch it.
Oh, you think the soul is some ghostly sheet,
Like things that fly around in the air,
That you can see through like smoke.

That's my soul lying there;
I put it there so you could touch it.
That time when I opened myself up to you,
And told you some things about me,
That I hadn't told anybody else,
That was me putting my soul out,
In the space there between you and me,
So you could touch it.

Or that time I got upset in the group,
When we were talking
And I said my parents didn't love each other,
When I was a child,
And I knew it as a child.
I used to cry about it a lot.
Now I'm 34 years old and I don't cry anymore,
But once in a while my eyes still water.
That was me putting my soul out there,
In the space between you and me.

God? Oh, I don't know God.
I mean I don't know the God who sits on a cloud,
And has a white beard and white hair,
Or knows everything, sees everything,
And controls everything.
But I know you.

Is that God in your face?
Is that love?
Well, that's my soul lying there,
I put it there so you could touch it.
And if you want you can ignore it,
And it will go away.
Or if you want, you can stomp on it
And it will bruise and turn rancid like an old banana.
Of if you want you can put your soul there next to it,
And touch it.
And if you do, there may be love – there may even be God.
(*Bruce Larson*)

Encouragement starts in the lifestyle of the encourager; words only confirm what the countenance reveals. Encouragement gives the church courage to fulfill her purpose and provides the willpower to live in grace.

CHAPTER TWENTY

BENEDICTION

Peace be to the brothers, and love with faith, from God the Father and the Lord Jesus Christ. Grace be with all who love our Lord Jesus Christ with love incorruptible. (Ephesians 6:23-24)

Years ago I served on a jury in a downtown Chicago courtroom. The defense lawyer approached the jury box to give a final argument. Summing up the case, he concluded by saying, "In a moment the prosecuting attorney will have one final opportunity to speak to you. I want you to remember what you promised me during jury selection. Make your decision only on the evidence." His comment left an indelible mark in the minds of all the jurors.

The final remarks anyone makes are the ones that usually leave the greatest impression. Paul, under the guidance and inspiration of the Holy Spirit, poured out his heart about the meaning of the church.

In the first part of the letter, the covenant-community is described. The Lord designed the gathering of believers to include divinely called leaders and devoted followers of Jesus. The *organism* is created like the human body, functioning best when everybody works in harmony with everyone else. The *organization* is a temple where people give honor to the mighty and merciful God.

The latter part of the letter reveals the nature of grace living and guides believers into reflecting Jesus accurately. They are committed to a life that shows tremendous worth in Christ, having been properly prepared by spiritual mentors. They also give honor to God by their home environment and work ethic. And they are properly equipped for battle against the spirit of the age, including prayerful vigilance. Finally, leaders keep those following Jesus moving forward by regularly expressing an encouraging word.

What more needed to be written? What summary remark would capsulate the exclusive concept of church? What closing thought did the Holy Spirit want the covenant-community to remember? The concluding appeal pertains to an *incorruptible love*.

Something corruptible eventually ends. Incorruptible love is an undying love, an everlasting love. Did these followers fulfill the final benediction?

Church historians think Paul wrote his letter around AD 62. As was highlighted in the introductory chapter of this book, John, a beloved member of The Twelve, recorded a supernatural revelation of Jesus. The special vision, written sometime near AD 95, began with a vivid description of the Christ and then documented the contents of various letters, sent by Him, to seven churches, one of them being Ephesus. How did Jesus describe this covenant-community some 30 years later?

"To the angel of the church in Ephesus write: 'The words of him who holds the seven stars in his right hand, who walks among the seven golden lampstands. 'I know your works, your toil and your patient endurance, and how you cannot bear with those who are evil, but have tested those who call themselves apostles and are not, and found them to be false. I know you are enduring patiently and bearing up for my name's sake, and you have not grown weary. But I have this against you, that *you have abandoned the love you had at first*. Remember therefore from where you have fallen; repent, and do the works you did at first. If not, I will come to you and remove your lampstand from its place, unless you repent." (Revelation 2:1-5)

Paul challenged them to keep *love incorruptible* yet, years later, Jesus criticized them because *first-love* was abandoned. How could this have happened in such a short period of time? Are there indications when love is corrupted and dying? Can it be avoided? Is this a path every church is destined to travel? Is it inevitable?

Paul's benediction shows a few indicators when love has a debilitating disease and death is on the horizon.

Love dies when *peace* is replaced with *quarrels*

"Peace be to the brothers" (V.23) is a statement of an *imperishable* love. When love is incorruptible, inner tranquility covers the heart and believers become undisturbed by diverse circumstances.

Peace is often lost when a few think Christ is no longer guiding the church, a feeling frequently occurring during difficult situations and trying moments. When believers recognize the Lord is always in control, peace is evident. No issue, within or outside the covenant-community, is too big for God.

A lack of peace will produce quarrels, a clear signal of a lost first-love. Quarrels arise by hatred, discord, jealousy, fits of rage, selfish ambition, dissensions, factions, and envy; the acts of the sinful nature. The conclusion is a disinheriting of His kingdom. (Galatians 5:20-21)

Grace living involves love, joy, peace, patience, kindness, goodness, faithfulness, gentleness, and self-control; the fruit of the Spirit. (Galatians 5:22-23) Developing and expressing these qualities coats first-love with an impenetrable shield, warding off harmful and fatal contaminants.

Your true character is often hidden deep inside, unseen, like soup carried on a tray high over a waiter's head. No one knows what is inside the bowl until the waiter is bumped and trips. Similarly, people will not know what is inside you until you are *bumped*. If the love of Christ is genuinely within, what spills out is grace, not griping.

Day-to-day living in today's economy is designed mostly around competition. People are expected to be highly aggressive, always pushy and relentless. Yet are believers supposed to be insistent and demanding with each other? Not hardly! They are loving the same God and walking the same road. "So then let us pursue what makes for peace and for mutual upbuilding." (Romans 14:19)

A lack of peace in a covenant-community is a sign of a damaged first-love and a distortion of grace living.

Love dies when *faith* is replaced with *deeds*

"Love with faith" (V.23) is a statement of an *indestructible* love. Experiencing the fullness of divine love requires faith.

Most everyone lives with the premise, "I will believe when I see!" Love for God is rooted in, "I will see when I believe!" No one can achieve a love relationship with the Lord by meritorious actions.

In Revelation, Jesus admonished the church at Ephesus about their deeds. (Revelation 2:5) No matter how commendable the toil, how astute the knowledge, or how prudent the activities, love for God must first be an encounter *with faith*.

In the classic movie, "Guess Who's Coming to Dinner," the white daughter of a socialite family brings home her fiancée, who happens to be black. Back when the film was released, this would have been the cause for a major stir in the average American home.

As the story develops, friends and family members from the homes of both the man and woman are troubled over the potential problems the future may hold for them. The young man's mother has a private conversation with the young woman's father on a back terrace. She ends up wondering, "What happens to you men when you grow old? When you men grow old you forget what it is like for a man to love a woman."

Have some believers grown so old in their relationship with God that they have forgotten what it means to love with faith?

Covenant-communities fail when they forget what made them dynamic; namely, taking bold actions out of deep-seated love for God. When love includes faith, not only is a beachhead secured but His reign increases and advances. The church must always take on an element of risk in order to bring the message of Christ to neighborhoods, cities, nations, and continents. Anything less is a malformed love, a mutant affection.

Was the church at Ephesus, 30 years later, simply trying to hold on to elements of past glory; a rich heritage, a unique distinctive, a glowing reputation? If so, the disease causing *dying love* was germinating within, ready and waiting to kill the body of Christ.

The Carson Pirie Scott building on State Street in

downtown Chicago was built using classic designs, showing majestic splendor and regal elegance. As the structure aged the infrastructure eventually corroded. The facility was starting to crumble. The restoration required supporting the outer shell with scaffolding while the inner supports were repaired and reinforced. Once the outside brace was in place, pedestrians had a sure-tale sign something was wrong inside. The problem with the building was no longer hidden beneath the surface and an overhaul was underway.

When the true meaning and value of church is crumbling, Jesus prefers to expose and aggressively attack the *corroding pride* that gloats over past achievements and yesteryear greatness. Very humbling yet incredibly restoring!

The remedy given by Jesus is *remember*, *repent*, and *redo*. (Revelation 2:5) Do once again activities *based* on faith, deeds *grounded* in faith, and actions *built* on faith. Show a love constructed with faith.

Warning symptoms of corrosion demand attention and should be quickly addressed. Yet some would rather crumble instead of face exposure and correction. Sad!

Love dies when *grace* is replaced with *law*

"Grace to all" (V.24) is a statement of an *everlasting* love. What creates sincere relationships is mercy! In grace living, *a love that forgives* has premier billing.

The twin of *grace* is *gratitude*. Gratitude replaces a

have to response with a *want to* desire. When serving God becomes a chore, first-love is lost. When delight changes to drudgery, desire changes to routine, and victory changes to struggle, then love has become legalized and grace is missing.

Consider a few "Do I have to…?" statements:

"Do I have to go to church?" *First-love* declares, "I want to go to church."

"Do I have to read my Bible and pray every day?" *First-love* declares, "I want to have time with God, reading His love letter, and talking with Him."

"Do I have to faithfully tithe and give offerings?" *First-love* declares, "He is Lord of everything connected to me. I want to give liberally and cheerfully."

"Do I have to be actively involved in ministry?" *First-love* declares, "I want to do for Jesus what I'm divinely gifted to do."

If a person loses gratitude, *have to* replaces *want to* and first-love fades from view; sometimes even leaving the heart. When gratitude is lost, grace reverts to law.

Abandoned first-love

The fruitful actions of believers residing in the covenant-community are rooted in first-love. May it never be abandoned! Hold on to *peace* instead of quarrels, *faith* instead of deeds, and *grace* instead of law.

Cherish and preserve a first-love for the Kingdom of God. Embrace incorruptible love, the true basis for the perfectly designed covenant-community and the sustaining pillar of all grace living.

EPILOGUE

BLESSING

These reflections began by stating an old *Irish ditty*. Hence, it seems quite appropriate to end by pronouncing a classic *Irish blessing*, given to every divinely called leader and devoted follower of Jesus:

May the road rise up to meet you.
May the wind be always at your back.
May the sun shine warm upon your face;
the rains fall soft upon your fields
and until we meet again,
may God hold you in the palm of His hand.

ACKNOWLEDGEMENTS

As a married student attending college, my involvement on campus was simply the classroom, the chapel, and library. The professors were extremely kind to give special attention to those with limited time for college life. The faculty giving instruction in Ancient Languages, Bible, and Theology helped to establish a greater clarity and deeper love for the Church. I am forever grateful for their instruction and encouragement, especially the following faculty:

Orville Clark

Donald Fee

Amos Millard

Daniel Pecota

John Pope

Jack Rozell

Francis Thee

Dwayne Turner

Maxine Williams

Thank you for not only loving the Lord but serving the Church by raising up developed and dedicated servants of the Lord.

ABOUT THE AUTHOR

S. Robert Maddox gave oversight for over 36 years to upper Midwest churches and briefly served in Higher Education. His work included elected positions within the Assemblies of God and other non-for-profit organizations.

Bob presently devotes time to writing and teaching. He publishes a weekly blog at *bob-maddox.blogspot.com* and has six additional books.

Bob is an ordained minister and nationally accredited volleyball coach, helping students and athletes develop a winning mindset and unbeatable life skills. He is passionate to see every generation enter into a life-changing relationship with God and become transformed followers of Jesus.

Bob and his wife Brenda raised four children in the Chicago area. Each one follows Jesus and utilizes their gifted abilities to advance the divine message of hope and grace.

OTHER BOOKS BY THE AUTHOR

SPIRIT Living, *abundantly following Jesus*

ACTION, *Reflections from the gospel of Mark*

GOD, *who are You?*

TEN Words, *Reflections from the Ten Commandments*

BLESSING and battles, *Reflections on the Blessing of God and the Battles of Life*

practical **FAITH**, *Reflections from James' letter to the Church*

Available in both Paperback and eBook editions.

62473941R00126

Made in the USA
Charleston. SC
16 October 2016